Any relationship is only as goo  without great communication levels of intimacy that God c enjoy. While *Honey, We Nee* resource for married couples, it also iii.iu..... for couples who are seriously dating or engaged. It's an easy read that goes beyond theory and clichés to practical tools and skills that can make an immediate difference in your relationship. This is a book that you'll read, refer to, and want to pass on to others.

—GARY J. OLIVER, ThM, PhD
EXECUTIVE DIRECTOR, THE CENTER FOR
HEALTHY RELATIONSHIPS
PROFESSOR OF PSYCHOLOGY AND PRACTICAL THEOLOGY,
JOHN BROWN UNIVERSITY

If you feel scared, tongue-tied, frustrated, or overwhelmed by the thought of having a heart-to-heart with your spouse, this book is for you. The level of communication in your marriage will skyrocket as you implement this proven advice. Plus the stories in this book are flat-out hilarious!

—ARLENE PELLICANE
AUTHOR, *31 DAYS TO BECOMING A HAPPY WIFE*

Honey, We Need to Talk by Dr. David Clarke confronts the greatest single challenge to marriages today—communication. He addresses the issue with enough candor, admission of personal failure, and humor laced through serious issues to make the "cure" palatable and even pleasant. Dr. Clarke brings professional expertise, experience, and biblical insights to bear on the issue of communication lapses. I also appreciate the fact that [the book] allows unmarried couples to confront their futures, evaluating where they are and making the decision to either marry or walk away from the relationship. I recommend *Honey, We Need to Talk* without reservation.

—HAROLD J. SALA, PHD
AUTHOR AND FOUNDER, GUIDELINES INTERNATIONAL

Honey, We Need to Talk

DAVID E. CLARKE, PhD
WITH WILLIAM G. CLARKE, MA

SILOAM

Most CHARISMA HOUSE BOOK GROUP products are available at special quantity discounts for bulk purchase for sales promotions, premiums, fund-raising, and educational needs. For details, write Charisma House Book Group, 600 Rinehart Road, Lake Mary, Florida 32746, or telephone (407) 333-0600.

HONEY, WE NEED TO TALK by David E. Clarke, PhD, with William G. Clarke, MA
Published by Siloam
Charisma Media/Charisma House Book Group
600 Rinehart Road
Lake Mary, Florida 32746
www.charismahouse.com

Cover design by Lisa Rae McClure
Design Director: Justin Evans

Visit the author's website at www.davidclarkeseminars.com.

Library of Congress Cataloging-in-Publication Data:
Names: Clarke, David, 1959- author.
Title: Honey, we need to talk / David E. Clarke, PhD, with
William G. Clarke,
   MA.
Description: Lake Mary, Florida : Siloam, 2017.
Identifiers: LCCN 2016052364| ISBN 9781629989679 (trade
paper) | ISBN
   9781629989686 (ebook)
Subjects: LCSH: Man-woman relationships--Religious aspects--
Christianity. |
   Marriage--Religious aspects--Christianity. | Interpersonal
   communication--Religious aspects--Christianity.
Classification: LCC BV4597.53.M36 C53 2017 | DDC
248.8/44- dc23
LC record available at https://lccn.loc.gov/2016052364

While the author has made every effort to provide accurate
Internet addresses and phone numbers at the time of
publication, neither the publisher nor the author assumes
any responsibility for errors or for changes that occur after
publication.

17 18 19 20 21 — 9 8 7 6 5 4 3
Printed in the United States of America

CONTENTS

WHY CAN'T WE TALK?

I LOVE THRILLER NOVELS. They always start out with a bang. That first dramatic sentence sends a chill up my spine, and I'm hooked.

> Mr. Smith didn't know it, but he had thirty seconds to live.

> The terrified woman and her paddleless canoe rushed toward Niagara Falls.

> The helicopter carrying the senator shuddered as the missile struck.

> As the glamorous actress left the hotel bungalow, the lone assassin raised his rifle.

This book you are holding is a *relationship* thriller. So I'm going to start out with my own dramatic sentence:

> I know the secret to deep, lifelong intimacy between a man and a woman.

I'm not kidding. I really do know the secret.

I *should* know it. I've been married to my beautiful blonde, Sandy, for over thirty years. Together we have learned a lot about intimacy. I've also been a Christian psychologist in

1

private practice, working with all kinds of couples with all kinds of problems, for over thirty years. That's a total of sixty years of experience with opposite-sex marriages!

The secret is this: learning to tell each other the truth about practically everything.

I say *practically* because there are some private matters that are only between you and God. I say *learning* because no one has the natural ability or inclination to communicate clearly and deeply with the opposite sex. No one. When we begin a relationship, we are not prepared or even able to be open and honest with the other person.

Quite the opposite, in fact. We hide the truth. We hold back the truth. We distort the truth. We have no idea how to truly connect in conversation and get to know each other.

Why? We don't speak the truth because it is human nature to protect oneself and not be vulnerable. Sharing truth, especially with the person we are closest to, exposes us to potential harm and pain. It feels a lot safer to keep truth hidden.

THAT SLIVER OF SOAP

A communication breakdown can happen so easily too. Here's just one example from my marriage to Sandy.

For the first ten years of our marriage, Sandy and I had no problems with our shared use of the bathroom shower. She showered in the evening, and I showered in the morning. Her shampoo was on the top shelf of the shower organizer; mine was on the middle shelf. She was in charge of buying her shampoo, and I bought my own.

Most important, we shared equally the replacing of the essential element of every successful shower experience: the bar of soap. Sandy always kept a good supply of soap in the hall closet, a mere ten steps from our shower stall. It was an unspoken agreement that we took turns putting a fresh bar of soap in the shower whenever it was needed. The soap bar rested in the place of honor on the bottom shelf of the shower organizer.

As I'm sure you know, there's really nothing worse in a shower than a sliver of soap. When a bar of soap reaches a certain level of *sliverness*, shall we say, it will not produce any lather no matter how hard you rub it. Instead, it splits into two or more pieces, and when you try to rub the pieces in your hands, they fall to the shower floor. Once the fragments hit the floor, the centripetal force of the water hurries them toward the drain.

Of course you quickly bend over and try to collect the pieces before they slide out of reach and become irretrievably lodged in the drainpipe. You fail and thus are forced to touch the slimy, hairy, incredibly nasty drain to clear it of the pieces. Your hands are now infected with the drain residue and eleven kinds of bacteria. But you can't wash them because *you don't have any soap!*

Sandy and I avoided this nightmare scenario with a highly effective procedure. Whenever the bar got down to a sliver, whoever happened to be about to shower at the time would walk to the closet and get a new bar.

We operated for a solid ten years on this guiding principle of shower etiquette. When faced with the dreaded sliver of soap, we followed seven simple steps out of respect for the shower component of our marriage:

1. Feel free to express the perfectly normal response of "Oh no! Not the sliver!"

2. Accept your fate with a wry grin, and realize it's no one's fault.

3. Turn off the water, and get out of the shower.

4. Throw the sliver into the wastebasket, because soap slivers are useless and a health hazard.

5. Wrap a towel around yourself, and walk the ten steps to the hall closet to get a new bar of soap.

6. Return to the shower with the new bar, and begin your shower.

7. Feel good—maybe even a little proud—that you have done the right thing and kept your marriage running smoothly.

As I mentioned, this sliver-of-soap replacement system (or SOSRS, if you will) worked beautifully for ten solid years.

Then one day it screeched to a sudden and horrible stop.

I will never forget the morning I stepped into the shower, got wet, and was faced with the dreaded sliver. I was shocked and appalled. I had taken a shower the previous morning and knew that I had used up the final suds of the bar. I had put the sliver back, knowing Sandy would replace it with a fresh bar that evening. I knew I had lucked out and that she would have to go through the seven steps of SOSRS.

But she hadn't replaced the bar! My showering world was turned upside down in an instant.

Being the gracious and loving husband I am, I decided to give Sandy the benefit of the doubt. Maybe she was stressed, caught up in the demands of caring for our three children. Yeah, that was it. I told myself this was just a onetime, out-of-the-ordinary occurrence.

So I replaced the bar and didn't say a word. I expected

her to say something appreciative like, "Thanks for putting in that new bar of soap, Dave. I blew it, and I'm sorry. You are a kind and thoughtful husband. Will you forgive me?" Instead, she said nothing. I was slightly concerned about her lack of response, but I let it go.

Then it happened again! And again. And again. Sandy had stopped replacing the sliver. She never said a word. She unilaterally decided she was through replacing it.

This was unfair. It was selfish. It was just plain wrong. I mean, who did she think she was? The Queen of England? Was I her sliver replacement boy? How dare she leave me with the sliver of soap every single time and act as though nothing was wrong! Apparently, she did not know with whom she was dealing.

I decided to fight back. Two could play at this game. I decided to wait her out. As the next bar of soap got smaller and smaller, I held the line. I knew she was expecting me to replace it. Dream on, baby! I was not going to do it. Not this boy. Not this time.

The sliver got down to a nub. Down to tiny pieces. Down to almost microscopic dimensions.

And Sandy still did not replace it!

I held out for a week. I abandoned the miniscule sliver and took extraordinary measures. I used shampoo to wash. I used hand soap from the sink. I am ashamed to confess that I even used a new bar for a few days that I kept in my underwear drawer.

In utter desperation I took the dramatic step of putting a new bar in its unopened package right beside the sliver. I had her now. All she had to do was to throw out the sliver, open the package, take out the new bar, and place it on the shelf.

But she wouldn't do it. What was the matter with her? Was she trying to send me to the mental hospital?

Finally, I confronted Sandy. It was mano a mano time. I walked up to her, holding the unbelievably small sliver of soap in my palm, and asked, "What do you have to say for yourself?"

With a fake confused look, Sandy replied, "What are you talking about?"

Oh, she was good. Very good. I had to give her that.

I told her the whole story of the sliver-of-soap replacement system and how she'd ruined it. She accused me of being crazy. Well, maybe I was, but she was the one who had driven me crazy!

Then she said, "Dave, weeks ago I switched from the bar soap to body wash. I haven't touched the soap. Didn't you notice the body wash container by my shampoo?"

Outraged, I replied, "No, I didn't notice the body wash! I thought it was a shampoo bottle. Why didn't you tell me you were switching to body wash?"

My spunky wife shot back, "I assumed you'd figure it out. Why didn't *you* tell me weeks ago about the sliver-of-soap issue?"

My point is we didn't talk to each other. We lived together in the same home for weeks and didn't talk about the soap issue. Just a few sentences would have prevented it from becoming a conflict.

Obviously the soap sliver was a very minor issue in our relationship. We weren't going to break up over it. But it is an example of what happens to every couple in the realm of communication. We don't talk to each other. Not on a deep level. No way.

When we do talk, we keep it superficial and safe. We

protect ourselves. It's too risky to speak specific, detailed, "Here's who I really am" truth.

We don't open up and talk honestly. We don't speak the truth on minor or major issues. We have a long list of things we don't talk about. We don't reveal how we really feel and think about anything important: our personal lives, our spiritual lives, the past, current struggles and problems, the relationship, dreams, the future...

It is the unspoken things that limit intimacy and eventually kill it. It is what we don't say that keeps us from the soul-mate closeness that we need and that God wants us to enjoy.

Most couples never break through to honest, revealing communication. As a result most couples never become genuinely intimate. The quality of your communication determines the quality of your intimacy.

If you want to take your relationship to a deeper level, it's time for real talk about real issues. That's where I'm going to take the two of you in this book.

HOW TO USE THIS BOOK

To achieve an authentic, robust closeness, you must learn to talk honestly and openly in ten essential areas:

1. Emotional intimacy

2. Spiritual intimacy

3. Conflicts

4. Past pain with others

5. Positivity

6. Needs

7. Areas of sin and weakness

8. Finances

9. Parenting

10. Physical intimacy

Why are these ten areas essential? Well, because I say they are essential. I'm the doctor, right? In all seriousness, in my experience, both professionally and personally, being honest in these areas will reveal who you really are inside. And when that happens, deep intimacy is the result.

In a hands-on, intensely practical workbook style, I will guide you and your partner through each of these ten essential areas. Each chapter will open with some general context about the subject at hand and then move into the same five practical components:

> How Are We Doing?—an initial block of questions that helps you assess how you are doing in the essential area covered in the chapter

> Here's What We Can Do—a teaching section, where you learn the relationship skills taught in the chapter

> What Will Block Us?—a second block of questions that helps you identify ways you might be hindered from working on this area together

> Let's Practice—instructions for how to put the skills into practice

🐦 How Did We Do?—a final block of questions
that helps you evaluate how you did when
you applied the skills

This book is a how-to road map to lifelong intimacy. My
process will teach you the key communication skills needed
for closeness and increase your proficiency as a couple in
these ten essential areas. It will enable you to talk intimately
about any topic for the rest of your life together.

Every step of the way I want you both to read each chapter
on your own. Then go through the chapter together and put
together your action plan. Talk through the initial "How Are
We Doing?" questions, make sure you're on the same page
about the steps I'm outlining for you to take, and then discuss the "What Will Block Us?" questions. After you take the
practice steps over a set period of time (usually a week), come
back together and answer the "How Did We Do?" questions.

On average it will take you three months to complete all
the chapters. Take your time. I bet you'd say your relationship is worth three months!

If you struggle with a chapter and don't feel able to work
through it as described, discuss your hesitation with your
partner. Then just move on to the next chapter. As you get
deeper into the book and learn more about yourself and
your partner, you may find yourself able to come back to
the difficult chapter and do the work.

This book is ideal for couples who are not married. If
you are seriously dating, engaged, or perhaps even living
with your partner, this process reveals far better than any
premarital test whether you can achieve full intimacy as a
couple. You will know with 100 percent confidence by the
end of the book if you ought to consider marriage or break

up. If you and your partner develop a greater degree of intimacy through this process, you can marry with confidence. You will be ready to live together as husband and wife, equipped to handle conflict and nurture real intimacy. But if you work through these ten areas together and do not achieve intimacy, end the relationship. Your relationship will have proven itself unable to reach a deeper level. (More instruction for unmarried couples is given in chapter 16.)

This book is also ideal for couples who are married. No matter how long you've been married, your journey through these ten essential areas can get you to the intimacy you're missing. I believe that if both of you are committed to the process and do your best each step of the way, God will bless your marriage with a special closeness. Your marriage is sacred to God, and He wants you to enjoy a forever, intimate love relationship.

However, if your spouse will not go through the entire process with you, I urge you to take a series of tough-love steps. (More on this too in chapter 17.)

Now, are you ready for real communication and real closeness as a couple? Good.

Let's get to work.

ESSENTIAL AREA 1

WE NEED TO TALK ABOUT OUR EMOTIONAL INTIMACY

CHAPTER 1

MEN ARE CLAMS,
WOMEN ARE CROWBARS

I'VE SPENT THE last thirty years observing thousands of couples and how they communicate with one another. Dating couples, engaged couples, living-together couples, and married couples. Couples who have been together just a few months and couples who have been married fifty years. Couples of all ages, cultures, races, and spiritual backgrounds. Couples with children and without children. Couples in biological families and couples in blended families.

What have I discovered about how couples communicate? When it comes to intimacy, one partner works hard to get it, and the other partner works hard to resist it. Since 85 percent of the time it is the woman who tries to create intimate conversations, that is the scenario I will follow in these three chapters dealing with emotional intimacy.

To illustrate this universal "I want intimacy/I don't want intimacy" communication pattern, I will now present two classic conversation scenes between a man and a woman. I include in these dialogues what each partner says and what each partner thinks but does not say out loud.

SCENE ONE:
"HOW WAS YOUR DAY?"

Woman: How was your day? [She's thinking, *Maybe something interesting happened that we can talk about.*]

Man: Fine. [He's thinking, *My day is over, and I just want to move on.*]

Woman: [She's thinking, *Fine? You've got to be kidding me. That tells me nothing. We can't build a conversation on "Fine." I'll try again.*] What happened today?

Man: [He's thinking, *I thought "Fine" covered it. It was just another day. Nothing special. The truth is my mind's a blank. I couldn't tell her what happened twenty minutes ago.*] Nothing.

Woman: [She's thinking, *Nothing? He went through an entire day and nothing happened? That's impossible! Why won't he open up and talk to me?*] Is there anything on your mind at all?

Man: You know, there is. What's for dinner?

SCENE TWO:
"WHAT'S YOUR RESPONSE TO WHAT I'M SAYING?"

In this scene the woman shares her personal information with the man with the hope that he will understand her better and share his own personal information in response. She talks about her day, the events and persons she finds interesting, her thoughts, and her feelings. She wants—and needs—his reaction to what she's saying. All I can say to her is, "Good luck."

Woman: [She talks to her man about a variety of things that happened during her day—places she went, people she talked to, and her feelings about all that happened. She's thinking, *I hope something I say will spark a response and we can have a conversation that goes deeper than just the facts.*]

Man: [No response. He says nothing. He's thinking, *Man, she's talking about a lot of stuff that I'm not really interested in. I can't keep it all straight in my mind.*]

Woman: [She's thinking, *Really? He has nothing to say about me and my day? Can he hear me talking? Does he need a hearing aid?* She talks about four or five other topics in an effort to get a response.]

Man: [Gives two grunts and a snort. He's thinking, *Not more information! I can't process what she's already said!*]

Woman: [She's thinking, *Now I know how a female gorilla feels. I need more than a few grunts and a snort! I need some conversation. Does he care about me? I'll try to be more direct.*] Any thoughts or feelings about what I'm saying?

Man: I don't know. [He's thinking, *Too many topics! Can't concentrate! Please stop talking. Or keep talking but don't ask me for a response, because I ain't got one.*]

Woman: [She's thinking, *What do you mean, "I don't know"? When do you think you will know something? I'm not sure I can wait that long. I'll give it another shot.*] What are you thinking about right now?

Man: Nothing. [He's thinking, *Nothing, except I wish you'd stop asking me all these questions I can't answer!*]

Woman: [She's thinking, *He has nothing on his mind? Nothing at all? Nada? He's either lying or needs more than a hearing aid. He needs a brain.*]

THE SAME OLD COMMUNICATION PROBLEM

Are these two scenes familiar to you? Oh, I know they're familiar. You're thinking, *Has this guy been recording our conversations? Can he read minds?* You've repeated these same lines over and over and thought similar thoughts, haven't you? Don't feel bad. All couples do.

Do you see the problem here? It's the same old communication problem that has plagued every couple since Adam and Eve: the woman presses for closeness, and the man resists her. She works her crowbar, and he keeps his clam shut. She wants him to know her more. He figures he knows her well enough. She wants personal, deep conversations. He prefers superficial conversations. She tries to get him to open up and share, and he keeps everything inside. (Note: In 15 percent of opposite-sex relationships, the woman is the clam. If this is the case in your relationship, it's entirely normal. Just walk through these chapters from the reverse direction. Mrs. Clam will be the one following the steps and learning how to open up.)

If you can't find a solution to this clam/crowbar dilemma, you'll never—and I mean never—have deeper conversations. Thus, you'll never have real intimacy.

I have the solution.

How Are We Doing?

- In your relationship, who is the clam and who is the crowbar?

- Crowbar, what are you thinking and feeling when you try to experience closeness?

- Clam, what are you thinking and feeling when you are pressed to open up?

- What is the clam/crowbar problem doing to your communication?

- Talk about these two scenes and how often they occur in your relationship.

HERE'S WHAT WE CAN DO

I have a simple four-step solution to the clam/crowbar predicament. These steps will generate more personal conversations and, therefore, more emotional intimacy.

Step 1: Have three thirty-minute Couple Talk Times each week.

If you don't consistently create time for communication, you can't communicate. Each weekend sit down together and schedule three thirty-minute Couple Talk Times for the upcoming week. Because the Bible teaches male leadership (Eph. 5:22–24), the man is responsible for scheduling these communication times and putting them on the calendar—yes, specific days and times—to make sure they happen.

Create a place in your home that is private, quiet, and comfortable. Allow no distractions—no kids, no pets, no television, no phones, no computers. If you don't share a home, use a quiet, comfortable room in one of your homes, or find a quiet, secluded spot, like a restaurant or a park. If you are in a long-distance relationship, use the telephone or Skype.

I want you to believe and embrace something right now: *Virtually all of your emotional intimacy will occur in these thirty-minute Couple Talk Times.* You can connect in a conversation only when you escape life and its distractions. True connection happens only under these conditions.

Step 2: The woman shares one-way, and the man reflects what he hears.

I want you ladies to feel free to talk to your men. That's what you already do, but I want you to talk in a specific way that I call *one-way communication.* One-way communication is sharing for ten or fewer minutes about one topic with no expectation of an immediate response.

This specialized style of female communication that I've developed (and which may win me the Nobel Peace Prize for doing so) effectively answers the two main male complaints about how women talk:

略 "She talks too much, and I get lost."

略 "She expects me to respond right away, and I can't do that."

Ladies, when you shift from topic to topic in one conversation, your man gets overwhelmed and his brain shuts down. He stops listening and goes into "the Zone." You've seen him there before—eyes glazed, mouth hanging open, dumb look on his face. The Zone is rude, but it's actually a form of self-preservation. You're talking too much for him to take in—and it's not football or cars—and his neural circuits get overloaded. Look, I've done the research. And I have been in the Zone myself.

In addition to using too many words, ladies, you want him to respond right away to what you are saying. He can't do that. I'm not kidding. A man simply can't quickly process and give an immediate response to what you're saying. He cannot travel the distance between his present thinking and your strange world that fast. He needs time—twenty minutes to twenty-four hours—to look inside and come up with a response that will move the conversation forward.

And if you pressure him for a response, he will certainly clam up and never respond to that topic. When a man feels controlled, it's conversational game over.

A woman, on the other hand, can and will instantaneously process everything you say and spit back a series of immediate replies. In fact, ladies, you and another woman can talk at the same time and understand everything being said! But when you're talking to a man, it's a whole different ball game. He may seem as though he has the conversational skills of an animal, but it's simply that he communicates differently.

So, ladies, here's what I want you to do.

During the three scheduled Couple Talk Times and at other random times of the day, talk one-way to your man about topics that interest you. You may communicate these in person or in a variety of other ways: texting, e-mail, voice message, or on the phone. Talk about one topic at a time, and talk for ten minutes or less. (Less is better.) Share what you think, what you feel, and anything else that comes to mind about the topic. You may even ask questions of him.

But here is the absolute, unqualified, not-to-be-questioned-or-denied key: *Share with the expectation that he will not respond to you in that conversation.* Chances are about 100 percent that it will be hours later and probably even the next day before you get a personal response to what you shared. Most of the time, his response will come later in a Couple Talk Time.

Also know he will not respond to every topic you bring up. He'll respond to selected topics that interest him in some way.

Knowing this, share topics in two categories. The first is the maybe-he'll-respond category. These are topics that interest you that your man may or may not (and probably will not) find interesting enough to give a response. Toss out these topics to him in ten-minutes-or-less blocks of time, and then leave it up to him to respond or not.

The second category, which should comprise 5 to 10 percent of all you say, is for the I-need-him-to-respond topics. These topics are of great interest or importance to you, and they're ones to which you really, really, really need to hear his response. Always flag these vital topics so your man knows that giving you a response is critical. Say something like, "Honey, this means a lot to me, and when you're ready, I need your response."

Men, there's something important you need to do when the woman you love is talking. You need to do it for both categories of her communication—the maybe-he'll-respond and the I-need-him-to-respond categories: you need to reflect back what she is communicating.

Now you don't necessarily need to give a personal response to what she has said. That comes later. Reflecting is telling her and showing her that you understand what she's saying. Reflecting is a form of active listening. When you reflect, you feed back key words and phrases concerning content (what she is saying) and emotion (how she feels about what she is saying). In doing so, you will help your woman feel heard and not just listened to. The practice of reflecting spells c-a-r-i-n-g to her.

In response to her statements you might say:

> ֍ "The doctor was late, and you were ticked."

> ֍ "The fight with your mom makes you feel sad and hurt."

> ֍ "The Bible study was great, and you feel at peace and close to God."

Part of reflecting is asking questions about what she is saying. Questions show you are interested in her. They also serve to clarify aspects of what she's sharing.

Men, reflecting provides you with three major benefits. One, it lets your woman know you are listening and interested in her life. Two, because of the first benefit, she will talk less. Three, it gets you engaged in conversation with her and prepares you to respond.

Step 3: The man processes and responds.

Now it's time for you, sir, to find, prepare, and deliver your personal response to the woman you love. It won't be easy, but I can teach you how to do it. She'll be happy—and if she's happy, you'll be happy.

In the course of a day, as we've already said, your lady throws out a bunch of conversation topics. She might do this in a Couple Talk Time, in the car, over lunch, or in a text or phone call. In addition to reflecting back to her what you've heard, your job is to identify those topics you find interesting and to which you plan to respond.

When you find an interesting topic or two out of all she presents to you, make sure you record that topic on a pad of paper or in your electronic device that you check regularly. Don't try to remember the topic; you don't have a memory. I'm serious about this: buy and use a pad for this purpose. It is all-important.

At some point when you're not in contact with each other, spend time processing the topic or topics that you wrote on your pad. At the same time, think of how you will respond. Ask yourself such pertinent questions as:

- What do I think about this subject?

- What does it remind me of in my past, in my family of origin, in my current life, or in my relationship with her?

- What emotions does it trigger in me?

- What could I tell her that would make her think and feel more deeply about this subject?

Dig deep. Think hard. Work to find your answers to these questions.

As you come up with responses to the topic, record them. Again, if you don't write down the thoughts and feelings you come up with, there's no way you'll remember them.

You may share your responses to the topic with your loved one at any time, but you'll probably wait until your next Couple Talk Time. That's the place where real communication and intimacy happen. During that Talk Time, refer to your notes and say, "Sweetheart, I have some thoughts about what you said yesterday" (and name the subject).

For the I-need-him-to-respond topics, follow this same procedure but know that you will *always record* these topics on your pad and *always get back to her* with your responses.

Step 4: Talk about a topic three times.

You are in the middle of your Couple Talk Time, and you—the man—have spent ten to fifteen minutes giving your responses to a topic the woman talked about earlier. What should you do now?

The woman will have a reaction to what you share, and maybe you'll have a reaction to what she says. So you go back and forth for ten minutes. Or after you give your reaction, maybe she talks for a while, and you reflect what she says back to her. You will probably need time to do more processing before you respond again. No big surprise there.

Here's what really gets you deeper: you're going to talk about this same topic in your next two Couple Talk Times. The initial cycle of communication, with the woman sharing, the man reflecting, and then the man responding, is only the beginning of emotional intimacy.

Then in the next few days, before your next scheduled Talk Time, I want each of you to process the topic and what has been shared so far. Come up with new reactions, new perspectives, and new emotions about the topic. The man will need to record his observations. The woman's amazing memory will probably allow her to do all the processing in her head.

In the next Talk Time you share more about the topic and go even deeper. Who knows what different and unpredictable places this conversation will take you? Likely your evolving reactions will take you far away from the original topic.

After this second Talk Time do more processing and continue the discussion in the third Talk Time. Now you're getting deep.

Talking about one topic in one sitting will never get you intimacy. Talking about one topic in three sessions, with both of you doing further processing in between sittings, *will* get you intimacy.

What Will Block Us?

- In the past, what has stopped you from communicating on a deeper level?

- What may get in the way of following these four steps?

- Which step will be hardest for you? Why?

- Where do you think you'll break down in the process?

LET'S PRACTICE

Have a meeting and schedule three thirty-minute Couple Talk Times for the coming week. Remember, the man is responsible for scheduling these meetings and calling the woman to the meetings.

Follow the pattern I have described:

> The woman shares for ten minutes or less on one subject.

❧ The man reflects back to her what he heard her say.

❧ The man chooses the topics from Couple Talk Times and other conversations to which he'd like to respond, writing them on his pad and processing his response before the next Talk Time.

❧ The two of you talk about these topics in all three Couple Talk Times.

How Did We Do?

- How hard was it to find a topic?

- Why was the topic interesting to both of you?

- What went well for each of you in the process of communication?

- What did not go well? Why?

- What will you do differently to improve your communication in your next three Couple Talk Times?

CHAPTER 2

IT'S TIME FOR
THE CLAM TO OPEN UP

A'AM, I HAVE to tell you something about your man. It's something you've probably suspected for years but couldn't prove. Even though this news will be distressing, deep down you've known it all along.

He'll deny it, but I guarantee it's the truth. And it will explain a lot about him and about your relationship. So sit down and get a strong grip on the armrest.

Your man is a CIA agent. The "job" he goes to every day is a front. A sham. A cover for his clandestine activities.

You know I'm right. The evidence, once you step back and look at it, is overwhelming. The man keeps secrets. He doesn't tell you much about himself, does he? You are on a need-to-know basis, and apparently you don't need to know much.

He doesn't talk about his job. He doesn't talk about his thoughts. He doesn't talk about his feelings. He doesn't talk about much of anything, does he? When you work for the Company, these are all matters of national security.

Did you ever wonder why he is such a master at avoiding your attempts to get him to open up and share himself with you? Well, now you know why. He's been trained by his CIA handlers to withstand brutal interrogations and keep his secrets inside. So when you are interrogating—I mean asking him to talk personally—he clams up tight and reveals nothing.

What's Going On?

All right, he doesn't work for the CIA. It just seems that way. But there are three central reasons your man doesn't share his secrets—his personal, inside self—with you.

He's a man

The first reason is simple. He's a man, and men are genetically engineered to avoid personal sharing—with a woman or anyone else. He wants to be in control, and personal sharing makes him feel out of control. He wants to project the image of a strong, capable man, and opening up makes him feel weak and vulnerable.

He is more logical and analytical than emotional. He sees the world through his logical lens and doesn't think emotions are helpful in coping with life and solving problems.

He also knows he's not good at this whole touchy-feely, intimacy thing. He figures, *If I'm not good at it, why try?* He wants to feel competent at tasks, and he feels incompetent in this realm of sharing personal thoughts and feelings. He believes he won't do well and that you'll be disappointed in him.

He's imitating the male role models in his life

Additionally he has never—and I mean never—seen another significant man in his life share something personal. Dad didn't do it. Stepdad didn't do it. Neither grandfather did it. Uncles, teachers, coaches, bosses—none of these influential men shared in a personal way in his presence.

What he did see these men do, over and over and over,

was stuff their emotions, act tough, and deal only in facts and logic. When they did talk, it was about sports and cars and politics and fixing things.

Is it any wonder he doesn't share personal thoughts and feelings with you? He was taught by other men to clam up and keep his personal information to himself.

A woman burned him

The third reason for his lack of personal sharing is that at least one woman in his past hurt him deeply. He loved her, he was close to her, and she traumatized him. It could have been his mother, a stepmother, a grandmother, a sister, a teacher, an old girlfriend, or an ex-wife.

That trauma caused him to put up thick walls around his heart, and he's not lowering them. He won't take the chance that you'll hurt him in the same way.

MAN, YOU HAVE TO OPEN UP

All right, Mr. Clam. I'm going to make this short and simple and clear. By not opening up and sharing personally on a regular basis with your woman, you are breaking her heart. She won't—in fact, she can't—feel loved by you if you don't reveal what's going on in your heart and mind.

She wants to know you. She wants to share your life. She wants to help you deal with your stresses and worries. She wants to know what you think and feel. She wants to be close to you—closer than anyone else. In fact, these are not just wants. These are her deep needs in your relationship.

When you learn how to share regularly with her on a personal level, you'll both experience the benefits:

➥ She'll feel loved.

➥ She'll love and respect you.

➥ She'll be drawn to you physically, and your sex life will be greatly improved (but don't stop reading here—there are three more benefits!).

➥ She'll be happy, so you'll be happy.

➥ You'll be healthier—physically, emotionally, and spiritually.

➥ You'll be blessed by God for meeting some of your wife's deepest needs.

How Are We Doing?

- Tell your woman the reasons you don't open up and share personally with her.

- Talk to her about the male models in your life, especially your dad. What did these important men teach you about personal communication with a woman?

- Talk to her about the important women in your life, especially your mom. What kind of relationship did you have with your mom as you grew up?

- What woman burned you in your past? Tell your woman what happened and how it has affected the way you communicate—or don't communicate—with her.

- Ask your woman how important it is to her for you to regularly share your inner life with her.

- Ask her what types of personal information she'd like you to share with her.

HERE'S WHAT WE CAN DO

I have a tool that will help you, Mr. Clam, open up and talk on a deeper, more personal level with your woman. This tool has helped me and thousands of men I've worked with in my therapy office, through phone and e-mail advice sessions, and at my marriage seminars.

What is the tool, you ask? It's called *the pad*.

You already know about the pad because I wrote about it in the previous chapter. I taught you how to use the pad for responding to topics expressed by your woman. Now I'm going to teach you how to use it to generate your own original, personal information.

Your woman loves when you respond to what she says. She also loves when you share your own personal stuff. The pad will help you do that.

Get a small pad of paper, and keep it with you at all times. Or use your iPhone or iPad. As you go through the day, record personal things about yourself that you think will interest your woman. Then talk about these personal items with her during your three thirty-minute Couple Talk Times.

You're thinking, *But what kinds of things do I record?* Good question. You have some idea now, though, because you just asked her that very thing when you tackled the "How Are We Doing?" section above. See that last item on the list? It's a prompt to ask her what type of personal information she wants you to share with her.

But I want to go further.

I'm going to walk you through a series of personal sharing categories. It has been my experience with my wife, Sandy, and all the women I've talked to as a psychologist over the last thirty years that these are the top ten areas in a man's life that hold real interest for a woman.

Events

Talk to her about events that occur in your day-to-day life. These could include work meetings; conversations with coworkers, friends, neighbors, or family; seminars; sporting events; and so on. If some interesting or funny piece of information came out of an event, record it.

Strong emotions

She's always asking you this really annoying question: "How do you feel about that?" You usually give the same old response: "I don't know." I know you're telling the truth, but aren't you tired of giving this lame response? Instead, be prepared. Beat her to the punch! Jot down the strong emotions you experience during the day—anger, frustration, joy, relief, hurt, fear, disappointment, peace—and share them with her.

Current stresses

Since I'm a man, I know what you think when you get stressed, and you don't want to talk about it with your woman. Here is a list of classic male excuses for stuffing stress and worry, and my responses:

Man: I can handle it myself.

Me: Yeah, you can, but your woman needs to be on the team, and she wants to handle it together.

Man: She doesn't need to know.

Me: She *does* need to know because your stress affects her.

Man: I don't want to upset her.

Me: She's as tough as you are, and she'll really be upset if you don't tell her.

Man: It's not that big a deal.

Me: It *is* a big deal because it's part of your life. No one else cares, but she does.

Man: Talking about it with her won't help.

Me: It *will* help! You can vent your stress, and she'll feel closer to you.

For the first ten years of our marriage I did not share my stresses with Sandy. Without meaning to, I hurt her and myself and our relationship. When I began telling her what was bothering me, I washed the stress out of my system—and we reached a whole new level of closeness.

Personal and relationship memories

As you go through your day sometimes memories from your past surface. You might remember moments about your childhood, family and friends, school, jobs, trips, joyful times, traumatic events, or illnesses. Sometimes the memories will be from your relationship—the honeymoon, vacations, funny events, children, moves, challenges, crises, or old friends you hung out with.

These memories, both positive and negative, are a gold mine for emotional intimacy. Many deep, satisfying conversations are about the past. Record your memories and share them.

Decisions

A typical man—me included—tends to think through a decision and come to a conclusion without ever talking about it with his woman. Bad idea for two reasons: (1) two heads are better than one when making a decision, and (2) you hurt her by cutting her out of the process. Tell her what you're thinking, and get her feedback every step of the way.

Your relationship with God

Your relationship with the Lord is the most important and personal part of you. Let her in! Tell her what's going on in your spiritual life, be it quiet times, insights from your Bible reading, ways you're applying the Bible to your life, ways God is guiding and directing your life, spiritual victories, spiritual defeats, topics you're praying about, your spiritual struggles, or your questions and doubts.

Your church experience

Every time you are in the house of God, you are impacted spiritually. God blesses you, communicates with you, changes you, and teaches you. How did the worship affect you? How did the sermon influence you? How did serving God at church change you? How did talking to and praying with others impact you? Share these experiences with her.

What you read and watch

Everything you read (books, articles, online material, newspapers, and magazines) and everything you watch (movies, television, and online video clips) can lead to a great conversation with your woman. Record your insights and reactions, and tell her.

Positive thoughts about her

Dwell on her personality, especially her character traits—traits like patience, love, sense of humor, kindness, strong work ethic, honesty, or spirituality. When she displays one, record it. Then in a Couple Talk Time, praise her for that trait and describe a few other times she has exhibited it.

Think about all she does for you (not to mention the kids and others in your life), and tell her what you've noticed about these sacrificial acts of service.

Observe closely and at least once every two weeks tell her how you think she's doing in her personal life. Is she happy, stressed, anxious, busy, fulfilled?

She'll love hearing what you think about her—who she is as a person, what she does for you and others, and how she's doing in her life.

Evaluations of your relationship

Your woman spends a lot of time thinking about your relationship. So when you evaluate your relationship and share how you think it's going, your thoughts will resonate with her. What are the strong areas, weak areas, things you need to improve, or things you'd like her to improve?

What Will Block Us?

- Which of these ten personal sharing categories will be easiest for you? Why?

- Which of the ten categories will be most difficult for you? Why?

- What will stop you from recording and sharing your personal thoughts and feelings in these ten categories?

- Ask your woman what she thinks will stop you.

LET'S PRACTICE

Sit down with your woman—today or very soon—and schedule three thirty-minute Couple Talk Times over the next seven days. Note these ten personal sharing categories on your pad or electronic device. Every day record personal information in at least one of these areas. It's OK to use one category more than once. Then share your recordings in all three of your Couple Talk Times.

How Did We Do?

- Tell your woman how you think you did with the "Let's Practice" exercise. What did you do well? What do you need to improve?

- What was most difficult about this assignment?

- Get your woman's honest assessment of how she thinks you did. What pleased her? What can you do better?

- Take what you shared this week and ask her how you can go deeper and be more revealing. What else does she want to know regarding how you think and feel about these items?

- Record what she wants, process it for a day or two, and get back to her with the results.

CHAPTER 3

PUT EVERY TOPIC
ON THE TABLE

I LIKE COUNTRY MUSIC. There, I said it, and I'm not ashamed of it. It's catchy, and it makes me happy. My favorite country music song of all time is the Alison Krauss version of "When You Say Nothing at All." It's a hauntingly beautiful song with a wonderful melody. I'm singing it right now as I write these words.

The song's main chorus line is "You say it best when you say nothing at all." And though I love the song, this line is probably the dumbest thing I've ever heard in my life. Actually, you say nothing when you say nothing at all. That's what *nothing* means.

Silence is not communication. You have to speak or your partner won't know who you are, you won't work through any issues, and you certainly won't create any substantial, permanent intimacy.

I'm sure you've heard that 80 percent of communication is nonverbal. As far as building deep, lasting intimacy goes, this is the second dumbest thing I've heard. Baloney! Eighty percent of communication is verbal. I'm sorry, but you have to open your mouths to communicate on a deeper level. You can't nonverbal your way through a conversation.

So with impeccable logic I have established that talking

is vital to your communication as a couple. It's my job to state the obvious.

But it's not just talking that leads to intimate communication and emotional intimacy. It's both of you being willing and able to talk about everything. No topic should be off limits. Genesis 2:24 describes marriage as the "one flesh" relationship. To be one flesh is to be in total and complete unity, literally being one in every area. You can't be one flesh—not even close—without total and complete honesty on every possible topic.

It you're not married, you are aspiring to be one flesh, and so the same principle applies. In fact, speaking honestly about all topics will give you the confidence and intimacy you need to seriously consider marriage.

HOW TO KILL A RELATIONSHIP

If there is even one topic in your relationship that you are not willing to discuss, that is what will kill your relationship. Stone-cold dead. Here are some examples from my clinical practice of what an undiscussed topic will do to a relationship.

"We didn't talk about his anger"

He wasn't physically violent, but he was verbally abusive to her. Often.

> **Woman:** If I bring up his anger, he'll have an angry outburst.

> **Me:** I bet he will. So what? He has them anyway. The only way he'll stop is by you making him talk about it and get help to fix it.

Result: She refused to bring up the issue. After ten years of tolerating his outbursts, she discovered her respect and love for him were gone. She divorced him.

"We didn't talk about her spoiling our child"

She gave their child everything and asked for nothing in return. The child, not her husband, was her top priority.

> **Man:** She's very sensitive about her mothering. She had a harsh mother, so she goes overboard with her love. If I bring this up, she'll feel rejected.

> **Me:** You mean in the same way you feel rejected by her? If you don't push her to address her own mom issues, your child and your marriage will be ruined.

Result: He chose not to talk to her about her growing-up years and her parenting of their child. They're still married, but it's a miserable and loveless marriage. And their child is an out-of-control mess.

"We didn't talk about his flirting and porn"

For years he flirted with other women and watched pornography.

> **Woman:** It's just too awkward and painful to talk about what he's doing. At least he's not having an affair.

> **Me:** If you don't talk about it and demand changes, your life will get more awkward and painful. Flirting and porn are serious sins, and in God's eyes he's already committing adultery. [See Matthew 5:28.]

Result: She did not talk about his behavior. He eventually found another woman, had a full-blown adulterous affair, and left her for this other woman.

"We didn't talk about her not meeting my needs"

For years he tried to be a good husband and followed the traditional Christian teachings: "Don't share your complaints, keep on loving her, and eventually she'll meet your needs." It didn't work because this approach never works. She figured he was happy because he didn't tell her he was unhappy.

> **Man:** I don't want to make a federal case out of this. I'm worried that bringing it up will make the situation worse.

> **Me:** It *is* a federal case! Some issues *are* federal cases! If you don't make this a federal case and bring it up, things will get a lot worse.

Result: He decided to avoid the issue. He finally hit the wall, lost all love for her, and divorced her. She was shocked and was willing to change, but he could not have cared less.

"We didn't talk about his lack of commitment"

They'd lived together for two years. She wanted to get married, but he didn't and wouldn't talk about it.

> **Woman:** If I bring it up, I'll lose him for sure. And I love him.

> **Me:** You've already lost him. Unless he is forced to deal with his lack of commitment, he'll never marry you. And if he won't talk about it, he doesn't love you.

Result: She kept bumping along for another year, hoping he'd commit. He never did, and she left him. By not bringing up the issue, she wasted another year of her life with a man who did not love her, and she suffered greatly in that year.

Whether to get married or not. Whether to have kids or not. Parenting. In-laws. Careers. Communication. The meeting of real needs. Sex. Money. Distribution of household chores. The location of your home. Addictions. Hurtful words and actions. Selfish behavior. Priorities. Feelings of loneliness in the relationship. Health. Hygiene. Lack of romance. Any pattern of behavior by your partner that has harmed you and the relationship. I could go on and on.

It is not these issues that kill your relationship. It is *not talking* about these issues that kills your relationship! If you don't talk about important issues, there will be no solutions. No forgiveness. No healing. And before you know it, no relationship.

How Are We Doing?

- Are there important topics in your relationship you haven't talked about? If yes (and if you said no, you are in denial), agree that it's time to talk about them.

- How has not talking about these topics affected your relationship?

- Sir, what topics do you want to talk about? Why haven't you pushed to talk about them?

> • Ma'am, what topics do you want to talk about? Why haven't you pushed to talk about them?

HERE'S WHAT WE CAN DO

Discussing difficult, sensitive topics is never easy. But it needs to be done, and it can be done. I have a five-step process that will help you talk through any topic in a healthy, effective way.

Step 1: Schedule the first meeting.

The partner who has an important topic to discuss goes to the other partner and schedules a time and place to start the process. Right up front, tell your partner the topic—no surprises—to allow him or her to get ready emotionally for the first meeting.

Use a neutral place in your home for these discussions. Don't use your bedroom or the warm, fuzzy location where you have your usual Couple Talk Times. Use a spot you don't care about, such as an office, a living room you rarely use, the kitchen table, or a back porch. If you're not living together, use one of your homes or a private place in public, such as a park, one of your vehicles, or a quiet restaurant.

Before the first meeting, you both must agree on one central ground rule: you will deal with only one topic at a time. All five of these steps will be completely focused on only one topic. No couple can successfully talk through more than one important topic at the same time.

Step 2: Have your first meeting.

If you're the partner who requested the meeting (the Speaker), you go first and make your presentation about the topic. This is a one-way conversation—a monologue. It is not a dialogue.

You share as completely as possible your thoughts, feelings, concerns, fears, questions, and any possible solutions.

If you are the "receiving" partner (the Listener), your job is to listen and reflect back what you hear. As your partner speaks, you work hard to communicate—through verbally feeding back key words and phrases and acknowledging what is being said—that you understand what your partner is saying and feeling. You may want to take notes as your partner is talking. Taking notes shows you care about your partner's point of view and want to answer all questions that are asked of you.

Step 3: Process your partner's position.

The listening partner takes a few hours, or maybe a few days, to process what the other partner expressed. You think about what was said, pray about it—that you will understand and have the right attitude—and prepare your response. Taking this time (which should not exceed three days) allows you to seriously consider your partner's position and invite God to provide guidance.

When you're ready, you go to your partner and schedule a second meeting.

Step 4: Have a second meeting.

Here you follow the same procedure as in the first meeting: one speaks and one listens. But now the roles are reversed as the Listener becomes the Speaker and fully expresses his or her thoughts, feelings, position, and possible solutions.

If you're the new Listener, you do your best to communicate—again through reflecting—your understanding of your partner's viewpoint and emotions on the topic. Go ahead and take notes so you don't miss the key parts of your partner's message.

Again, as the Listener you don't give your response. You just listen and understand.

At the end of the meeting, if you both feel ready to do so, schedule your next meeting, which will focus on solutions. This meeting could happen immediately, several hours later, or later in the week.

Step 5: Have a final "solutions" meeting.

At this point in the process both partners have fully expressed their positions, emotions, needs, desires, and potential solutions connected to the topic. Just as important, both feel heard and understood.

In this solutions meeting you are now ready and able to engage in dialogue. While there is still one Speaker and one Listener, reactions and opinions are shared more rapidly. Once the Listener has reflected back what has been said, he or she may respond immediately.

At the beginning of this solutions meeting you may want to share additional information and emotions if needed. Sometimes you will need to vent your emotions more or further clarify your position. Get this additional expression out, ensure that understanding is taking place, and move into solution mode.

Take turns proposing ways to solve the problem. Brainstorm together. Look for compromises. For some issues one solutions meeting may be enough. For more difficult issues you will need several meetings.

What Will Block Us?

- What will stop you from talking about difficult, awkward topics?

- What do you fear will happen if you do address these topics?

- Is there a deep, personal reason you're not ready—or able—to discuss a certain topic? What is the topic, and what is your reason for not being ready?

- If you're not ready, are you willing to enter individual or couples counseling—as soon as you have completed this book—to get past your personal obstacles to dealing with the topic?

LET'S PRACTICE

Go through my five-step process twice with two different topics. Take one topic at a time. The first topic will be one the woman selects. Why? Because as the servant leader (see John 13:3–5), the man should aim to meet his woman's needs. After talking though the woman's topic, the man will select his own topic, and the two of you will repeat the process.

If the topics you choose are complicated and extremely sensitive, you will need more than a few days to get through the process and reach effective solutions. For deeper wounds you've suffered from your partner, you'll need a month or more to complete this process. But at least you will have started the process and made some progress.

If necessary, take a break from the book to thoroughly talk through these tougher topics. Or put these topics on hold, complete the rest of the book, and then return to these topics and work through them to a conclusion.

How Did We Do?

- What was most difficult for you in the five-step process?

- Do you feel you made significant progress with the topics you chose to talk about?

- At what point did you get bogged down and struggle? Why did you struggle?

- Are you both willing to commit—right now— to keep on talking about these topics until you reach a satisfactory conclusion?

- Are you willing to commit—right now—to always talk through any topic your partner wants you to address?

- Have you not forgiven your partner for a hurtful action or hurtful pattern of behavior? Will you both agree to address this wound using the five-step process?

- Are you willing to commit—right now—to always talk through any topic your partner wants you to address?

ESSENTIAL AREA 2

WE NEED TO TALK ABOUT OUR SPIRITUAL INTIMACY

CHAPTER 4

WHERE ARE YOU WITH JESUS?

WHEN THEY BOTH were sixteen years old, a boy named Chaz wanted to date my oldest daughter, Emily. I should say *man* instead of *boy* because Chaz was a six-foot-eight-inch, three-hundred-pound mountain of muscle who played offensive lineman for his high school football team.

Chaz could have put me in a headlock and said, "Dr. Clarke, I'm going to date your daughter. What are you going to do about it?"

But he didn't do that.

Instead Chaz went through "the interview." Emily and her siblings (Leeann, Nancy, and Will) had known for years that anyone who wanted to date them would have to be interviewed by Dad a week before the potential date, at least while they were in high school. I even told all four kids the questions I would ask the punks—I mean young persons—who showed up for the interview.

Chaz and I sat down in the dining room. He was nervous and looked like he was about to wet his pants. Frankly, I enjoyed the feeling of power.

I asked him a series of questions as I cleaned my shotgun. OK, I wasn't cleaning my shotgun. But my questions were tough.

I asked him about his grades. His behavior at home and at school. Alcohol and drug use. How he treated his mom.

49

Other girls he'd dated. (None, luckily for him.) The college sports teams he rooted for. (The University of Florida Gators had better be on the list.)

But the most important questions came first and were about his spiritual life:

- Are you a Christian?

- What makes you a Christian?

- Are you growing in your relationship with Jesus Christ?

- What are you doing to grow in this relationship?

- Do you regularly attend a local church?

- Do you regularly attend this church's youth group?

- Do you have a daily quiet time in which you pray and read the Bible?

You're thinking, *Really? Were you expecting him to be the next Billy Graham?* As a matter of fact, yes. Yes, I was. That's the kind of man I wanted for my three girls. That's who I want—and who God wants—for all single ladies.

I want a godly young woman for our son, Will, too. I want her to be the next Sandy Clarke (my wonderful wife) or the next Ruth Graham. I hope and pray this is the kind of woman Will wants to date and marry. This kind of spiritually healthy woman is who I want—and who God wants—for all single men.

Chaz passed the interview with flying colors. He had a good relationship with Jesus, was an outstanding young man, and treated Emily like a queen. He treated her so well, she married him. They gave us our first grandchild, Isabel. I've already told Isabel, who's almost three, "Watch out for the punks of this world, baby! You want a man like Daddy."

Leeann, Nancy, and Will learned from this first interview. They never brought any unqualified dating candidates to Dad for the interview. Leeann and Nancy also have married fine Christian young men (Andrew and Phil). Will, who is at the University of Florida (go, Gators!), remains on the market.

WHY SPIRITUALITY IS SO IMPORTANT

The two most important qualities to look for in a romantic partner are spiritual: (1) the person has a personal relationship with Jesus Christ, and (2) he or she is growing in that relationship. Of course, these need to be true of you, the one seeking a lifelong partner, as well.

Once you become a couple, these two governing life principles remain vitally important for the duration of your dating time and your entire marriage. The other nine areas covered in this book are essential for the health and intimacy of your relationship, but your spiritual lives will determine the success or failure of it.

Why is this true? If you don't know Jesus personally, or if you know Him but aren't growing in your relationship with Him, you are living life in your own human power. And that power is extremely limited.

With no supernatural help, you are doomed to fail in your personal life and in your relationship with your partner. On your own, you can't apply what I teach in these ten areas. You can try, but it won't work.

Unless you both have a strong, growing relationship with

Jesus, you also will be unable to develop a spiritual bond as a couple. If Jesus isn't at the center of your personal lives, He isn't at the center of your relationship. Spiritual intimacy is the deepest, best kind of intimacy, and you won't be able to experience it.

WHAT MAKES YOU A CHRISTIAN?

I'll make this simple because the Bible's message about how you become a Christian is simple.

There is one God, and that is the God of the Bible. There is one way to establish a relationship with God, and that is through His Son, Jesus Christ.

Here is Jesus Christ, in His own words:

> I am the way, the truth, and the life. No one comes to the Father except through Me.
> —JOHN 14:6, MEV

A Christian is someone who has a personal relationship with God through Jesus. God sent Jesus to die for your sins—all the things you've done wrong—so that you can have a relationship with God:

> For God so loved the world that He gave His only begotten Son, that whoever believes in Him should not perish, but have eternal life.
> —JOHN 3:16, MEV

Here is what you must believe to become a Christian:

> For I delivered to you first of all that which I also received: how Christ died for our sins according to

the Scriptures, was buried, rose again the third day according to the Scriptures.
—1 CORINTHIANS 15:3–4, MEV

When you believe these three truths—Jesus died for your sins, He was buried, and He rose from the dead—and ask Jesus to be Lord of your life, you become a Christian. You have a personal relationship with God through His Son, Jesus. You have power to improve your life and your relationship with your partner, which will bring you a joy and peace you have not had. Plus, and this is a big plus, you're going to heaven when you die.

How Are We Doing?

- Do you have a personal relationship with God through His Son, Jesus?

- If not, what is keeping you from beginning this relationship?

- If you do have this relationship, rate it on a scale of one to ten (one being very healthy and vibrant and close, and ten being very unhealthy and distant).

- What is going well in your relationship with Jesus?

- What is not going well, and what is keeping you from improving your relationship with Jesus?

HERE'S WHAT WE CAN DO

If you're not a Christian yet, I urge you to become one. You can begin your relationship with God through Jesus right now by saying the words in this brief prayer—but know that it is not the saying of the words that makes you a child of God; it is the intent of your heart:

> *Dear God,*
>> *I know I am a sinner. I've made many mistakes and sinned in my life. I realize my sin separates me from You, a holy God. I believe that Your Son, Jesus Christ, died for my sins, was buried, and rose from the dead. I give my life to You now.*

If you prayed this prayer, I am thrilled for you. And God is thrilled. But if you're not ready to commit your life to Christ, here's what I want you to do. First, read Lee Strobel's book *The Case for Christ* or watch a DVD version. Lee presents a compelling argument for who Jesus Christ is and how He will change your life and your eternity. Discuss the book and/or the DVD with your partner.

Second, read the Gospel of John. This book of the Bible will introduce you to Jesus in a personal and powerful way. After reading it, discuss it with your partner.

Third, attend a local church with your partner for at least one month. After that month, meet alone with the pastor to discuss Lee Strobel's material and the Gospel of John. Get the pastor's input on Jesus.

These three steps will allow you to explore the claims of Jesus Christ and will give you the opportunity to make a decision about Him. The best decision you can ever make is to begin a relationship with Jesus! I'm just saying. But that's up to you.

If your partner isn't a Christian

If your partner isn't a Christian yet—whether you're married or not—work through these two chapters on spiritual intimacy together. In fact, work through the rest of the book together. I think there's a good chance that by the end of your work on these ten essential areas, your partner will want to become a Christian.

If you want to grow closer to Jesus

Four behaviors are critical to growing closer and closer to Jesus. As both of you live out these behaviors, you'll also grow closer and closer to each other.

The first is to have a daily quiet time with Jesus. During this time it's just you and Jesus, spending ten to fifteen minutes together in a private, quiet place. Use part of this time to pray, which means talking to Jesus. You can confess your sins, ask for His infusion of power to help you eradicate sins from your life, thank Him for all He's doing for you, share your triumphs and your troubles, and make requests. Also read a few verses of the Bible in a version that clearly speaks to you, and spend a few minutes meditating and thinking about how you can apply the Bible's truths in your life.

The second behavior is to pray throughout your day. Jesus is with you everywhere you go, so keep talking to Him. Tell Him what's happening, what you're thinking and feeling, when worry and anxiety creep in, and how you can see Him guiding you. Ask for His help, His wisdom, and His strength as you navigate the ups and downs of your day. (See Philippians 4:6–7; Colossians 2:2–3; James 1:5; and 1 Peter 5:7.)

The third behavior is to attend a local church every week. The Bible teaches that we are to be part of a local church (Heb. 10:25). But don't just attend. Get involved! Join a small group, such as a Sunday adult Bible fellowship class, a regular weekly Bible study, a life group, a Celebrate Recovery group, or a marriage group. And find a place in your church to serve others.

The fourth behavior is to have a spiritual coach. You can't grow close to Jesus on your own. Your spiritual coach should be a person of your own sex. He or she can be a close friend, an older mentor, or a younger person. Ask your partner who he or she thinks would be a good coach for you. Pray with your partner about who you can ask to fill this role. If you can't think of anyone or those you ask say no, ask your pastor to find you a coach.

Once you have identified the individual, here's how you ask this person to be your coach: "I want my relationship with Jesus to get better and deeper. I'm asking you to help me do that. Please meet with me in person once a week. We can do this by phone on the weeks we can't meet." In these meetings, have your mentor ask you about the following:

- How you're doing in your relationship with Jesus

- What actions you've taken to improve this relationship

- Insights you've gained from your Bible reading

- Your spiritual struggles and victories

&* What you're praying about in your quiet
times with Jesus

&* How last week's church service impacted you

Ultimately your coach will hold you accountable, support and encourage you, pray with you, and stand with you in the tough times.

Your partner (whether he or she is a Christian or not) also should help hold you accountable spiritually. I would encourage you to ask him or her to discuss the same questions with you each week. If both of you are Christians, this practice will help draw you closer. If only one of you is a believer in Jesus, these times will create opportunity for you to discuss spiritual matters, which will affect every area of your life, from how you handle money to how you raise your children.

What Will Block Us?

- I hate to be a pest, but I must ask you again: Are you ready to begin a relationship with Jesus?

- What will stop you from taking the three steps to faith that I recommended—reading Lee Strobel's materials, reading the Gospel of John, and attending a local church for a month?

- If you aren't yet a Christian, are you willing to talk to a pastor or a Christian you know and get answers to your questions about Jesus?

- If you are a Christian, what do you notice stops you from (1) having a daily quiet time, (2) praying throughout the day, (3) attending a local church and getting involved there, and (4) having a spiritual coach?

- If growing in your faith is difficult for you, has something painful happened to cause you to back away from Jesus, church, and other Christians?

LET'S PRACTICE

If you're not a Christian yet (notice I keep using the word *yet*—that's because I believe you will become a Christian!), read the Gospel of John this week and discuss it with your partner. Also, go to church with your partner this week and discuss the experience together.

As I suggested, in the next four weeks read Lee Strobel's *The Case for Christ* book or watch the DVD, attend a local church, and make an appointment with the church's pastor to talk about Jesus. As you follow through on these actions, talk about each one with your partner. You may take a break from this book to do these steps or work on them as you continue the book's process.

If you are a believer, practice these three spiritual behaviors this week: have a daily quiet time, pray throughout the day, and attend a local church. Whether your partner is a Christian or not, discuss these experiences as a couple. Also this week, think and pray about what small group in your church you can join and how you can serve there. And consider whom you can ask to be your coach. (Remember, you need to choose a person of the same sex.) In the next month take action in these areas.

How Did We Do?

- If you are not a Christian, what is your reaction to the Gospel of John? What are your impressions of the book and what it says about Jesus? How do you feel about the church service you attended?

- If you are not a Christian and your partner is a Christian, ask your partner why it is so important to him or her that you begin a relationship with Jesus.

- If you are a Christian, how did your daily quiet time go this week? What went well and what did not go well?

- If you are a Christian, did praying throughout your day prove easy or difficult? Why? What small group are you thinking of joining, and what area of service looks like a good fit for you?

- If you are a Christian, what is the one action you can take that will bring you closest to Jesus?

CHAPTER 5

HOW TO KEEP GOD AT THE CENTER OF YOUR RELATIONSHIP

*D*ID YOU EVER have a car you hated? I mean really, truly hated? Well, I did. My old four-door Saturn was the object of my loathing. That car—and I use the word loosely—was the bane of my existence.

I bought the Saturn for my two younger daughters, Leeann and Nancy. They needed a rattletrap to practice their driving. It was a safe car, but it was ugly and old and nobody cared if it was damaged in an accident.

Through a series of strange circumstances *I ended up with the Saturn!* It wasn't supposed to be my car. It was a car for two teenaged girls learning to drive. I already knew how to drive. It wasn't a car for a grown man with some self-respect and a fairly successful career. No!

For four years I drove the Saturn. Or rather, it drove me...nuts! It was old (did I mention that already?), it had rust stains and a variety of dents, it had worn and stained seats, the ceiling insulation hung down in poofy sheets, and the engine ran like a tank. (I've actually driven a tank, so I know how one drives.)

The engine ran incredibly rough—coughing and sputtering and wheezing—and the horrible sound it made was so loud I had to crank up the radio to ninety decibels. Of course—and this will shock you—the radio got three stations and they were filled with static.

Finally, one day my desperate prayers were answered when some guy rear-ended me. Sure, I got whiplash, but the Saturn was totaled by the insurance company. I still send the guy who hit me a Christmas card every year.

That car was worth about four dollars, but I got a check for about two thousand dollars. I felt I'd robbed a bank and gotten away with it.

It was time for a new car, so I went to see my son-in-law Chaz Weissing. He was a car salesman, and he owed me because I let him date Emily. After showing me a couple of sad, dingy cars (a classic technique), Chaz walked me over to the car of my dreams: a beautiful, sleek—well, sleek compared to the Saturn—champagne-colored 2004 Toyota Camry. It took my breath away. (It doesn't take too much to take my breath away.) It sported a pristine body, a nice interior, electric windows and doors, and cruise control. But best of all it featured a smooth ride and an engine that purred like a Persian cat. It was quiet and I could hear the radio—which got many stations.

The difference between the two cars was astounding. Dramatic. And delightful. I couldn't believe how happy and energized I felt driving my new—well, actually used— Camry. Compared to the old Saturn, the Camry made me feel like I was driving a Rolls-Royce. When I left for work in the morning, I'd tell Sandy, "I'm going to work now in my new car."

Welcome to Your New and
Greatly Improved Relationship

If you're not bonding spiritually as a couple, what you have is the relationship equivalent of my old Saturn. Even if your relationship is very good and you're happy together, it is nothing compared to what it could be with spiritual bonding.

I'm offering you—really, God is offering you—the Rolls-Royce of relationships. God wants you to experience the ultimate in intimacy, and for that to happen, you need to make Him the most important Person in your relationship.

You're thinking, *OK, I'll bite. I want the best relationship possible. What is spiritual bonding?* Here's my definition:

> Spiritual bonding is consistently placing God at the very center of your relationship and growing ever closer to Him as a couple.

This kind of bonding involves tapping the unlimited power of God and putting it to work in your relationship. When you are in a spiritual bond, you are no longer loving your partner in your own power. You now have God's power to love.

The Best Kind of Intimacy

If you base your relationship on physical intimacy, it will last six months to two years. That's it. Sexual attraction alone, as important as it is, is not enough to sustain a relationship. Two years into our marriage, Sandy and I lost a big part of our initial physical passion. Frankly, I blame the children.

If you base your relationship on emotional intimacy, it

will last four to seven years. Even if you work hard at communication, sharing openly and honestly, your emotional connection will weaken and eventually disappear. Seven years into our marriage, Sandy and I lost our emotional passion. Frankly, I blame the children. (Do you see a pattern here?)

The truth is it wasn't our four kids who killed our physical and emotional intimacy. These areas of intimacy died of natural causes. It would have happened without kids. Physical and emotional intimacy were not designed by God to last. They get us together in a relationship, but alone they do not carry us forty or fifty years down the road.

So what form of intimacy will carry you forty or fifty or sixty years? Spiritual intimacy—between the two of you and God. If you base your relationship on spiritual intimacy, it will last a lifetime. It will last as long as you both live.

About twelve years into our marriage Sandy and I realized we'd lost the physical and emotional spark. That was not acceptable to us. We didn't get married to have an "OK" marriage.

We admitted to each other that our lack of intimacy was not due to the children. It was not due to my demanding career or the busyness of our lives. It was because we had no spiritual intimacy.

We were both Christians, we attended church every week, and we had our individual quiet times with God. But since we were not sharing our spiritual lives with each other, our "Christian" marriage was not intimate. We were drifting apart.

It dawned on us that God was the answer to our intimacy problems. Why? Because God is the answer to all the problems we face in life and in relationships. The Bible says

"God is love" (1 John 4:16). God is the only source of love, including the love between a man and a woman.

When my wife and I began to bond spiritually, practicing the two actions I will describe in this chapter, we got our intimacy back. First, we developed spiritual intimacy, which is the best and deepest love possible. But it didn't end there! God took our spiritual intimacy and used it to energize our physical and emotional intimacy.

For the past twenty years we have experienced ongoing and deepening levels of all three kinds of intimacy: spiritual, physical, and emotional. If you and your partner will bond spiritually, you will come to enjoy great intimacy in these three areas as well.

Before you read further, one brief message. If one of you is not a Christian, go ahead and work through this chapter together. These spiritual bonding actions can move the non-Christian partner closer to making a decision to trust Jesus and begin a relationship with Him.

How Are We Doing?

- How many couples do you know who have lost their physical and emotional intimacy and split up?

- Have you lost your physical intimacy?

- Have you lost your emotional intimacy?

- How important is God in your relationship? Is He at the center?

> • Do the two of you talk about your individual spiritual lives on a regular basis?
>
> • Do you pray together on a regular basis?

HERE'S WHAT WE CAN DO

Remember the thirty-minute Couple Talk Times I described in chapter 1? (By the way, I hope you continue to have these Talk Times throughout your relationship.) There are two spiritual bonding actions I want you to do during each Couple Talk Time. These actions will connect you spiritually and give you a deep, permanent intimacy.

Action 1: Share your individual spiritual lives.

Take five minutes of each Couple Talk Time to tell your partner how you're doing in your relationship with Jesus. Share in detail what's happening in your spiritual life.

🕊 Descriptions of your daily quiet times

🕊 Insights gained from your Bible reading

🕊 Ways you're applying the Bible to your life

🕊 Spiritual victories

🕊 Spiritual defeats

🕊 Spiritual doubts and questions

🕊 Areas of temptation

🕊 Ways God is guiding you day by day

Don't be general. That's a waste of time. Be honest and be specific. Sometimes you'll talk about the exciting, positive things God is doing in your life and how close you are to Him. Sometimes you'll talk about how you are struggling with God and feel distant from Him.

Remember the spiritual coaching I mentioned in the previous chapter? This is that spiritual coaching in action. You are encouraging and supporting each other in the most important area of life. On your own you cannot experience significant spiritual growth. Real, deep spiritual growth always occurs in the context of relationship.

If you are not a Christian yet, you can still talk to your partner about how God is working in your life. He is doing things to bless you, to show Himself to you, and to get your attention and motivate you to begin a relationship with Him.

I think you can see that this kind of spiritual talk is very personal and intimate and requires courage. It is more intimate than sex. It will create a strong spiritual bond. It will also create a strong emotional bond through the interesting, stimulating, and revealing conversations it creates for the two of you. And your spiritual and emotional intimacy will lead to better-than-ever physical intimacy.

Action 2: Pray together regularly.

Take another five minutes of each Couple Talk Time to pray. List your prayer requests and your reasons to thank God—you can jot them down on the pad if you want—and decide which ones you each will lift up to God in prayer. Then hold hands and pray out loud, one at a time.

At first you'll pray for safe topics: your children, your family, health concerns, careers, your church, and people you know. As you go along, you'll start sharing about and praying for more personal, intimate issues, such as your worries, your fears, your dreams, your spiritual weaknesses, God's guidance in your life, and protection from Satan's attacks.

You'll never have a bad prayer time. You'll never say, "Boy, that was lousy. I wish we hadn't prayed." That's impossible. It will always be a sweet, precious, and powerful time of intimacy—with God and with each other. Honest praying is literally miraculous in drawing you closer to each other and helping you understand each other better.

God blesses you for praying together, and—here's the best part—He will answer your prayers!

> Again I say to you, that if two of you agree on earth about anything they ask, it will be done for them by My Father who is in heaven. For where two or three are assembled in My name, there I am in their midst.
> —MATTHEW 18:19–20, MEV

Sandy and I have had many of our joint prayers answered. Hundreds of couples I have worked with have prayed and seen answers. When God says He will answer the prayers of two gathered together, that's exactly what He will do!

One final note: it's common for one partner to feel awkward about praying out loud. No problem. It's OK for this partner to pray silently for two weeks. If you are the uneasy one, when you're done praying silently, just squeeze your partner's hand so he or she knows you're done. After a few weeks, you likely will feel comfortable enough to pray out loud.

What Will Block Us?

- What are your main concerns about sharing your personal spiritual life with your partner?

- What are your main concerns about praying together?

- Did your parents pray together as a couple?

- Have you ever prayed—on a regular, intentional basis—with a member of the opposite sex?

- What do you think will happen when you do share your spiritual life and pray with your partner?

LET'S PRACTICE

In your three thirty-minute Couple Talk Times this week, share what you have learned in your individual spiritual lives this week for five minutes, and pray for five minutes. As I mentioned in chapter 1, the man is responsible for scheduling these talk times and making sure they happen. Additionally, in this week's practice I want the man to share his spiritual experiences and thoughts first and to pray first.

Expect these two actions to be awkward and difficult at first. I am asking you to go way outside your comfort zones. But I am also offering you a gold mine of intimacy—a degree of intimacy few couples experience. It's worth it. Go for it.

How Did We Do?

- How tough was it to implement these two actions—to share your spiritual lives and to pray together?

- What did you find most difficult about these actions?

- Which partner struggled more, and why?

- What was the result of your doing these two actions together? How did you feel afterward? Did you feel closer to your partner? Did you feel closer to God?

- Are you both willing to continue sharing your individual spiritual lives and praying together?

ESSENTIAL AREA 3

WE NEED TO TALK
ABOUT OUR CONFLICTS

CHAPTER 6

FIGHT WITH CONFIDENCE

*I*F YOU'RE IN a romantic relationship, you will have conflict. After the first six to eight months of infatuation-fueled bliss, conflicts will begin to surface. Periodically your partner will annoy you, frustrate you, make you angry, hurt your feelings, and generally drive you nutty.

This is completely normal. It's supposed to happen, and it will happen. This kind of conflict doesn't have to do with the big, nasty, awkward issues I covered back in chapter 3. Rather, I'm talking about the basic, regular, day-to-day conflicts that impact every couple.

If you handle these normal conflicts poorly, you will end up with a dead relationship. It won't die immediately; it will die over time, a slow, agonizing death. Every time you fail to resolve a conflict, you grow a little further apart. Eventually you are miles apart and no love is left.

If you handle your conflicts well, you will achieve an intimate relationship. Your disagreements create sparks and relational intensity, which, if handled correctly, produce deep emotional connection. Every time you successfully work through a conflict, the two of you will be a little closer to each other. Each resolved conflict brings a greater knowledge of each other, which results in a greater love for each other.

The stakes are high, aren't they? You must learn how to fight with confidence and skill.

YOUR DYSFUNCTIONAL CONFLICT PATTERN

Every couple has a dysfunctional conflict pattern. You tend to handle every conflict the same way, and it is not an effective way. Your conflict pattern prevents you from even getting close to dealing with the real issue. The conflict conversation breaks down very quickly, and you are left with another unresolved conflict.

Here are five classic dysfunctional conflict patterns. See if one of them fits you and your partner.

One talks, and one shuts down

One partner really wants to talk about the conflict, but the other partner refuses to engage. It's a monologue, not a dialogue. The talker tries to get a response, fails, and finally gives up in disgust or despair. You can't make someone talk who doesn't want to talk.

Both avoid conflict

This is massive dual denial in action. Both partners know there is a conflict but act as if there is none. Nothing about it is ever mentioned. Both partners pretend there is no elephant in the living room. This approach is wonderful acting but poor conflict resolution. The conflict seems to go away but doesn't really go away.

One yells, and one retreats

One partner is the yeller, launching into a high-volume rant about the issue. The other partner, who hates high-volume ranting, immediately tries to get away from the yeller. The non-yeller will not talk about the issue, will not listen, and will leave the room as quickly as possible. If the yeller follows—which is often the case—the non-yeller will get behind a locked door or leave the house for a while.

Both yell

When a conflict occurs, both yellers immediately start yelling. Each yeller tries to outyell the other, hoping to win the argument by shouting down the opponent. Of course, no one is listening, so no progress is made in the conflict. Both yellers become increasingly angry and frustrated until, finally, one runs out of steam and stops talking.

One is logical, and one is emotional

One partner (usually the man) presents an airtight, logical case. At least it seems airtight to him. He briefly covers the key points and reaches a conclusion. He refuses to listen to his woman because she is emotional. He discounts her feelings, will not accept her feelings, and explains away her feelings. She, of course, becomes even more emotional, which causes him to further discount her position. The result? Zero conflict resolution and one angry and deeply hurt woman.

The Damage Is Done

Every time you engage in your dysfunctional conflict pattern, you get the same four results. First, you don't resolve the conflict. Second, you grow a little further apart because your intimacy level goes down and your walls of self-protection go up. Third, all your negative feelings fester and turn into bitterness and resentment. (These destructive emotions do not diminish over time; they strengthen.) And fourth, every unresolved conflict, along with its accompanying negative emotions, transfers to every new conflict.

Know this: when you have a conflict today, it is not just about that conflict. It's about all your unresolved conflicts from the past too. All this baggage makes it very difficult, if not impossible, to work through any new conflict that comes along.

Can you see the terrible damage your unresolved conflicts are inflicting on your relationship? If you don't learn how to deal successfully with conflict, you will be miserable or break up.

How Are We Doing?

- Which of the five dysfunctional conflict patterns fits your relationship? If yours isn't covered on the list, how would you describe it?

- What damage has your conflict pattern done so far in your relationship?

- How do you feel after you go through your conflict pattern cycle?

- In your previous romantic relationships, what was your conflict pattern?

- How did your parents handle conflicts?

HERE'S WHAT WE CAN DO

As I'm sure you've noticed by now, I have a plan for everything. For your normal, everyday conflicts, here is my seven-step fight-with-confidence plan. (These steps are similar to the steps I gave you in chapter 3 for discussing big, difficult topics. The main difference is that you'll be able to move through these more quickly.)

Step 1: Identify and stop your old pattern.

When a conflict erupts, you will immediately launch into your old, dysfunctional, self-defeating conflict pattern. You can't help it. It's automatic. One partner has to say as quickly as possible, "We're reverting to our old pattern, and we need to stop." Once this warning is given, it has to be honored.

Step 2: Schedule your conflict discussion.

You've stopped your old conflict pattern in its tracks. But you're not ready to talk yet. Anger and hurt are intense, and you will say and do things you'll regret.

Schedule a time to sit down and deal with the subject of the conflict. If you set it for even five minutes later, you'll be in much better shape to begin the discussion. It may be thirty minutes later, two hours later, or five hours later. If at all possible, start the discussion by the end of the day.

Choose a location in your home that is private, quiet, and neutral. Don't choose the bedroom or the special, cozy place you use for your usual Couple Talk Times. Use the kitchen table, the living room you seldom sit in, an office, or the back porch.

Step 3: Pray.

After you schedule your conflict discussion, each of you should go to a private place to calm down and pray for God's help in dealing with the conflict. Even a few minutes will help you simmer down and get ready to talk.

Step 4: Express yourselves one at a time.

When you are seated in your conflict-resolution location, one partner goes first. That person shares his or her feelings, thoughts, and point of view about the disagreement. This person is the Speaker, making the other partner the Listener.

Communication must proceed with one person talking at a time. There will be *one* Speaker and *one* Listener at all times. There must be no interruptions whatsoever when a Speaker is talking; the Listener will get his or her turn and be afforded the same courtesy. If the Listener speaks during the Speaker's turn to talk, the Listener is not really listening but is thinking about what to say, and thus no understanding is taking place.

Let's say, in this instance, the Speaker is the woman. In a block of ten minutes or less, she shares her opinion, feelings, and position—her "truth." The Listener's job is to say nothing at all during this time but only to *listen, accept,* and *understand.* The Speaker, meanwhile, should try to hold to the ten-minute rule, summarizing her feelings in one statement at the end of the ten minutes.

When the Listener has a turn to respond, he says only what will help the Speaker feel understood. He doesn't introduce any new thoughts but merely reflects back what the Speaker has said and validates her feelings, ensuring that the Speaker feels understood. For example, the Listener might say:

> You're angry because I came home late and didn't call to let you know.

When I said _____, you're saying it made you
feel _____.

Don't move on until the Speaker is satisfied that the
Listener understands and the Speaker *feels* understood.
What is essential is that the Speaker feels the other partner
truly understands.

When the Speaker tells the Listener she feels understood,
take a break for a minimum of ten minutes. Let the understanding you just created settle in and take root.

After the break return to your seats and reverse the roles.
The Listener is now the Speaker. In ten minutes or less, he
now shares his point of view, his thoughts, his feelings, his
truth—and that truth is going to be different and just as
important and legitimate as the other's truth.

Again, don't move on until the new Speaker feels understood by the Listener and says so.

You don't have to agree; in fact, very often you're not going
to agree. But you need to acknowledge and accept uncon-
ditionally the feelings of your partner. ("I don't understand
why you feel this way, but I accept your feelings and will act
accordingly.") You need to build an understanding of your
partner's feelings and position.

You may need some follow-up conversations in this stage.
Sometimes one time through is enough. Sometimes it's not.
If it's not, you need more one-at-a-time conversations.

It's common for the woman to need to do more processing to feel reassured that the man understands her. If
she's unsettled and doesn't feel understood, the conflict
cannot be resolved. So, sir, let her keep talking and clari-
fying, and work hard to communicate your understanding

to her. A few extra talks, with breaks included, can make all the difference.

Step 5: Make a deal.

Before you start this stage, take another break. This break can last from a few minutes to half a day or more. When both partners are ready to resume, agree on a time and return once again to your conflict-resolution location.

If you must decide on some course of action, such as a financial decision, a parenting strategy, a family scheduling change, or an agreement on something you want your partner to do or not do, you will need to work together to make a deal. With most of the anger gone and a substantial amount of understanding achieved, you will be in good shape to negotiate and reach an agreement.

At this stage you can probably go back and forth without utilizing the Speaker-Listener roles. But if things begin to get too intense, go right back to those roles and to the rules governing them.

Before you begin, take a minute or two to pray together for God to guide you to a good decision.

The deal you make must be specific and measurable. Don't be vague. Be willing to compromise. Sometimes your partner will agree to do it your way. At other times you will agree to do it your partner's way. At times you'll meet in the middle and work toward a compromise. Every deal is reached on a trial basis. If it doesn't work, either partner may call a meeting to renegotiate.

Step 6: Stop and start.

When a conflict conversation gets off track—even a little— shut it down immediately. When something goes haywire— for example, when one of you reverts to your dysfunctional conflict style—you can't save that conversation. No couple can. It's over.

Either person may call for a stop, and it must be honored. Take a time-out and get some space. It might be just five minutes. Go to the bathroom. Walk the dog. Suck down an energy drink or some hot tea. If you are the one who asked for a pause, tell your partner you'll let them know when you're ready to resume, or ask them to come find you when they're ready to resume. When both of you are ready, sit down and start up where you left off.

Step 7: Make sure you make up.

You've worked hard to talk through the conflict. You're relieved, and you feel closer to each other. You deserve a special reward. What kind of activity would be a fitting way to celebrate your successful resolution of the conflict? Getting ice cream cones? High-fiving each other? Reading the next chapter in this book?

No. Physical activity—that's what I'm talking about!

If you're not married, have a make-out session. If you are married, and it's a mutual desire, have make-up sex. The physical passion you can experience after working through a conflict together is intense and wonderful.

What Will Block Us?

- Of these seven steps, which will be the most difficult for you? Why?

- What are you afraid you will do to mess up the conflict-resolution process?

> • What are you afraid your partner will do to
> mess up the process? Tell your partner what
> makes dealing with conflicts so difficult
> for you.

LET'S PRACTICE

Pick a recent—or fairly recent—conflict that you didn't resolve. Discuss and work through this conflict together, following the seven steps. If you've never had a conflict in your relationship, find a topic you disagree on—even something minor—and go through the steps. Practicing these conflict-resolution skills is vitally important. Do it right now.

If you are not married, do not contemplate marriage until you have successfully resolved at least three conflicts. Knowing how to successfully resolve conflicts is a huge component of a happy marriage.

How Did We Do?

> • What was the most difficult part of the
> conflict-resolution process? Why?
>
> • Where did you get bogged down in the seven
> steps?
>
> • What could you have done differently to
> improve the process? What could your
> partner have done differently to make the
> process easier for you?

- Are you both willing to commit to following this seven-step process for all your day-to-day conflicts?

ESSENTIAL AREA 4

WE NEED TO TALK
ABOUT OUR PAST PAIN

CHAPTER 7

WHO'S ON YOUR PAST-PAIN LIST?

*I*F YOU THINK the chapters so far have been tough, you ain't seen nothin' yet. This chapter and the next are very difficult, but working through them can make a huge difference in your relationship.

We're going deep! The action steps in these two chapters are not for the fainthearted. If you want real intimacy, you have to do real work.

FIRST, THE BAD NEWS

OK, I'm going to cut to the chase. All your unresolved pain connected to past relationships is transferring to your significant other. You don't want it to, but it is happening on a regular basis.

Though unintentional, certain words and behaviors of your partner trigger memories of the unresolved pain caused by other persons. When this happens, your past pain automatically ignites and gets focused directly on your partner. Suddenly your partner is not just receiving your anger and hurt for whatever *he* or *she* did but also catching it for what others have done to you.

It's not just the two of you in this relationship, dealing with each other and the typical issues that come up between a man and a woman. That's hard enough. Often your past, unresolved pain leaks into your present relationship, preventing you from resolving problems and becoming genuinely intimate.

Here are some examples of past pain and how it can transfer to a current relationship.

The unaffectionate mom

His mom was a good mom who met his basic needs, but she was not an affectionate person. She didn't touch him much as he was growing up. No hugs. No kisses. No holding him on her lap. He has a deep need for physical expressions of affection from his wife, but she is not an affectionate person by nature either. Each day that goes by without her affection increases his hurt, frustration, and resentment.

The critical dad

Her dad frequently criticized her weight, her behavior, the way she performed her chores, and her choice of friends. For years she tried to gain his approval, but all she got was more criticism. Now when her boyfriend criticizes her—even low-key comments about small things—this old father wound is touched, and she sinks into a depressive, irritable state for days.

The cheating spouse

His ex had an affair and left him for the other man. He never got over the pain and feeling of betrayal. In his new relationship he is not able to trust his partner. He is suspicious of her relationships with other men. He wants to know where she is at all times. She is getting tired of his questions and controlling behavior.

The sexual abuser

She was sexually abused by an older neighbor boy. She never told anyone and never recovered from that trauma. Even though she loves her husband, she can't completely give herself to him emotionally or physically. Sex is not a happy, passionate experience for her. It's a chore.

The passive dad

His dad was a very passive man who let his mom run the household and make all the decisions. In his current relationship this man is passive and forces his wife to make the decisions. She needs him to step up and lead, but he resists. She's losing respect and love for him.

The selfish ex

Her ex ignored her and her needs. He focused on his career and his hobbies. He didn't talk to her and didn't spend time with her. All she was good for was taking care of the kids and sex. Now when her new man shows even a small hint of her ex's behaviors, she reacts with intense anger. Her frequent overreactions are driving this good man away.

Do you see how it works? I could give you a hundred examples of past-pain transfer. Everyone transfers. *Everyone.* Every significant wound in your past, if unresolved, will transfer to your current partner. And as you can see from my examples, the transfer does tremendous damage to the relationship.

In this chapter I'm going to help the two of you answer four critically important questions:

1. Who hurt you?

2. How did this person or these persons hurt you?

3. How does this hurt transfer to your partner?

4. How do you recognize what is happening and stop the transfer?

AND NOW FOR THE GOOD NEWS

The good news is you can heal from your past pain and eliminate its transfer to your partner. It is not easy work, but you can do it.

The best way to achieve healing is to heal together. I want you to go through the steps outlined in this chapter even if you've already recovered from your past pain with the help of a therapist. Including your partner in the process will ensure that you won't transfer that pain to him or her. And going through the process together will create a deeper level of intimacy for you as a couple.

How Are We Doing?

- Can you relate to any of the six examples above of past pain transfer?

- How did your mom and your dad, intentionally or not, hurt you as you grew up with them?

- Besides Mom and Dad, who else hurt you in your past?

- In what ways have you healed—through professional therapy or pastoral counseling or a recovery group—from your past significant wounds?

- Which of your past wounds are causing the most problems between you and your partner?

HERE'S WHAT WE CAN DO

Did I use the word *process* in the previous paragraph? You know I did. Does that mean I have a plan for you two to eliminate your past-pain transfer? You know I do.

To begin healing from your past pain, I want you both to take two actions. The first is to make a list of all who have caused you significant pain. That's right—actually write down the names. Maybe your mother hurt you, or your father. A stepmother or stepfather. A brother or sister. A cousin. An aunt or uncle. A grandparent. A foster parent. A boyfriend or girlfriend or other close friend. A fiancé or fiancée. An ex-spouse. A neighbor. A teacher. A coach. A Sunday school teacher or youth leader. A pastor. A child. A boss. A counselor. A fellow employee.

All of us have a list of those who have harmed us. Sometimes the harm done was intentional. Sometimes it was unintentional. Either way, the wounds of your past count, and they stay inside you until you clean them out, stopping their damaging effects.

Pray, both on your own and with your partner, that God will reveal the names of the persons who hurt you and the specific hurts they caused. Pray also that God will help you work through the pain of your past.

The second action is to sit down with your partner and through a series of conversations talk through each name on your list. Describe how the person hurt you, being as specific as possible about what happened. You won't heal without expressing the details.

What I am asking is for you to relive these memories. I know it will be painful and perhaps the last thing you want to do. But it is essential. Don't let feelings of false guilt or humiliation stop you.

Express how you feel about what was done to you—your emotions and your pain. I use the word *feel*, not *felt*, because your emotions are still inside you and still as fresh as when you first experienced them. If tears come, let them come. If rage erupts, let it erupt. If you feel deep hurt and sadness, let these emotions flow out of you. No holding back.

Do not—I repeat, do not—in any way spare those who wounded you. Do not make any excuses for their behavior, including accepting any blame for what they did:

> ح "Well, my dad had a bad childhood."

> ح "My mom was under a great deal of stress."

> ح "My neighbor had mental health issues."

> ح "Really, it only happened a few times, and it could have been worse."

> ح "This person had some positive qualities."

Do not rationalize, justify, or sugarcoat what happened. No damage control here. No efforts to make it seem as though your hurts are not as serious or as painful as they truly are. These are all attempts to minimize your pain, and they will keep your pain intact and operating at full strength.

Face what happened head-on, and describe the events and your feelings with total honesty. Dump out your raw, visceral pain. Truth heals.

Also tell your partner how you think the stored painful actions affect you and your relationship. How did your wounds change you? How do they affect you and your treatment of your partner? How do they shape your reactions to certain behaviors of your partner?

Ask your partner to answer these same questions. You may miss insights that he or she will notice. Two heads are better than one, and you are working together to help each other heal.

Keep in mind that you are not even close to forgiving these persons who damaged you. Not in this phase of the work. With the Lord's help you will forgive each person on your list because the Lord Himself instructed us to do so (Matt. 6:14–15). It is necessary for your healing. But forgiveness comes at the *end* of this process.

Right now, just describing the events and venting your emotions is a key step toward forgiveness. At this point it is important for you to fully express your pain. Forgiveness is not merely an intellectual choice; it is also a psychological and spiritual experience. When you do this extremely hard work, God will enable you to forgive.

You may be thinking, *Am I going to have to confront any of the persons on my list?* My answer is no. Not to achieve the purposes we are after here. We're focused only on healing, forgiveness, and elimination of the insidious damage that past-pain transfer can have on your life and relationships.

All three of these goals can be achieved without dealing directly with those who harmed you.

Moreover you first must heal and forgive before you can even think about confronting any of these persons. And God, working through a Christian professional therapist or your pastor, will show you if you need to confront, whom you need to confront, when you need to confront, and how to confront.

What Will Block Us?

- What is your reaction to these two difficult steps—making a list of all who have hurt you and talking through what happened in detail with your partner?

- Share any reasons you don't want to take these steps.

- What are your concerns, fears, and anxieties about making your list and talking through your past pain?

- How have you coped with your unresolved pain up to this point in your life?

- How has your past unresolved pain affected your close relationships?

- What will be most difficult for you about doing these two steps?

LET'S PRACTICE

This is it. I want both of you to sit down and make your list of those who have harmed you in the past. Then when you both have your lists, schedule private times to talk out the painful memories, your emotions, and the impact these events are having on your relationship with your partner.

This process may take just a few days, or it may take a week or two. It could even take several months of conversations that involve the repeating of memories if one or both of you have suffered serious traumas.

I urge you to take the time needed to work through these past traumas. They are alive inside of you and are causing all kinds of ongoing damage to you and all your close relationships. You can't ignore them away. With God's help and your partner's help, you have to work through them to make them go away.

If you have experienced deep wounds and therefore deep trauma, you may ultimately need to work with a licensed Christian therapist. A trained and caring professional therapist can make a huge difference in your healing. Include your partner in the therapy process so you can heal together. Keep your pastor—and I do hope you have one—updated on your work. Your pastor's prayer and support will be invaluable.

To find the best local therapist to work with you through this process, ask your pastor or call Focus on the Family at 1-800-A-FAMILY (1-800-232-6459), Monday through Friday, from 6:00 a.m. to 8:00 p.m. (mountain time).

How Did We Do?

- What was the worst part of going through these two steps?

- What was the best part? The most helpful part?

- Which person on your list caused you the most pain and damage?

- When you did the second step, did you get all the key details and all your emotions out?

- If you got bogged down in the process, where did it happen and why?

- Was your partner supportive as you did your work? If so, say it. Tell your partner how he or she can be even more supportive as you continue this process in the next chapter.

- Do you feel closer to your partner now?

- Are you willing to see a Christian therapist if needed?

CHAPTER 8

SPEAK THE TRUTH IN LETTERS

*T*HAT LAST CHAPTER was rough, wasn't it? Are you hanging in there with me? Believe me, this hard work is going to pay off for the two of you and your relationship.

Here's where we're going next in the processing of your past pain. I've been a therapist for thirty years. For most of those thirty years, I've had my clients write letters to those who have hurt them. If you see Dave Clarke in therapy, you're going to write letters. I believe so strongly in letter writing that if a client refuses to write letters, I won't continue to see that person in therapy.

Talking through your unresolved pain in past relationships is the first step toward healing. You did that in the last chapter, so you are on the way to full recovery from your internal pain and its transfer to your partner. But you're not done yet.

You know where I'm headed, don't you? You're thinking, *Oh, great. He's going to ask me to write letters to the individuals on my past-pain list.*

Yes, I am.

WRITING IS HEALING

Something about writing out your emotional pain is essential to a full and genuine recovery. When you write to a specific person, you make the direct confrontation that is necessary for healing. When you write, you are forced to face your pain and express it in an intensely personal, detailed way. Your words on the paper bring your traumatic life experiences from a dark, shadowy world into bright, clear reality.

Writing these letters will hurt. Really hurt. But it will also heal you and complete the process of eliminating your past-pain transfer to the one you love. And here's more good news: you won't be sending these letters. They are to be read only to your partner (and your Christian therapist, if you have one).

When I ask clients to write these letters, I never get this response: "Hey, that's a great idea. I can't wait to do it." They immediately realize how grueling and painful this step will be. They launch into resistance mode and try to get out of the homework.

Here are the most common attempts to avoid the writing of these letters and my responses:

> **Client:** I'm a terrible writer.
>
> **Me:** We're not going to publish these letters. Don't worry about grammar, spelling, or punctuation. Just write the truth.
>
> **Client:** These events occurred a long time ago. I don't think I can remember what happened.
>
> **Me:** Nice try. Your memories are intact, believe me. Start writing and the details will come back to you. God will give you the memories you need.
>
> **Client:** I've already healed and forgiven these individuals. I'm good.

Me: You may have forgiven them intellectually, but that's much different than emotional forgiveness. Writing these letters will move you toward complete healing and total forgiveness.

Client: I'm afraid this writing will stir up too much pain and I won't be able to handle it.

Me: If you don't write the letters, your pain will remain inside and do serious damage to you and your relationship with your partner. The letters will get the pain out and it will be gone for good. And you aren't doing this alone. You have God, your partner, and me to help.

I recently worked with two female clients who had been verbally and sexually abused by their fathers. They had carried this pain for years and struggled with poor self-esteem, depression, and anxiety. They could not fully trust their husbands or enjoy sex.

One wrote a letter to her dad and was healed as a result. She was able to forgive her father and move on with her life. The other did not write a letter to her dad. And she continued to be miserable and unhappy in her marriage. As you might imagine, I'd strongly encourage you to write the letters.

How Are We Doing?

- Have you ever written an honest, detailed letter to someone who hurt you? If so, did the writing help you clean out your emotions?

- If you sent the letter, how did the person respond?

- Have you kept a diary or a journal of your life events and relationships? If so, how has this writing helped you?

- Are you willing to keep an open mind as I explain how to write these letters?

Here's What We Can Do

In this chapter, I want each of you to take three action steps: (1) write a letter to each person on your past-pain list (many of my clients end up writing five to seven letters, but write as many as you need); (2) read the letters to your partner; and (3) schedule follow-up talks about these letters. Plan to take at least two weeks (maybe even three) to complete these three steps. One partner may write five or six letters. The other partner may write two or three. That's OK. Every person has a certain number of letters to write. Take as much time as you both need to work through this step.

Step 1: Write the letters.

Now you're going to write real letters with whole sentences and paragraphs. No lists or bullet points here. A full-fledged letter is more likely to reveal the truth about these important relationships, the pain you experienced in them, and the ways they impact your relationship with your partner today.

Again, these letters are *not to be mailed*. I want you to write them as if you were going to mail them. But their content will be shared only with your partner. Each letter will contain three parts. Part A covers the pain you experienced with the person and the behaviors you learned as a result. Part B deals with forgiveness. Part C describes the specific transfer you know has happened in your current relationship because of this previous relationship.

Part A: The pain and the learned behaviors

As you sit down to write, pray that God will give you what you need to put on paper. He knows what you need to express in order to heal and stop the pain transfer.

This first section of each letter is devoted to the honest expression of the pain the person has caused you and the dysfunctional principles you were taught about relationships because of it. Feel free to mention positives, but don't spend much time on them. It's the negatives that must be exposed. It's the negatives in these past relationships that are causing real problems in your current relationship.

Describe the person's personality, your relationship with the person, the person's weaknesses and shortcomings, and the ways this person hurt you. Select a few painful memories and write what happened and the emotions you experienced. If you made mistakes, mention them also.

You may be surprised—as many of my clients have been—at the amount of pain these letters will bring to the surface. Memories from years ago can still carry deep emotional power. Your emotional response as you write your letter—and later, as you read your letter—is a good indicator of how deeply you were hurt and where you are in the process of resolving these issues. Let your emotions flow freely. Healing comes through facing painful events and fully expressing your emotions connected to these events.

As you write about what happened and your emotional reaction to it, include what you believe the person taught you about relationships. What incorrect, ineffective learned behaviors developed out of your painful interactions with this person? For example:

- "You taught me to always stuff my emotions and pretend everything was OK."

- "You taught me that the way to handle anger is to raise your voice and rant and rave."

- "I learned from you that I have to perform if I want to be accepted and loved."

- "Dad, you taught me that men will always disappoint me, so it's not worth trying to trust them or let them get close."

Put down on paper—in detail—the pain these persons caused you and how the pain has damaged you and your relationships. Doing so will wash the pain out of your heart and mind and kill its power over you.

Part B: The forgiveness

In Part B write words of forgiveness. You've taken the critical step toward forgiveness by honestly expressing the way this person hurt you, your emotions about it, and the impact it is having on you and your relationships. Now it's time to let go of your resentment and bitterness and to forgive. Choosing to forgive someone is a huge step toward eliminating transfer from that person to your partner.

Previously I mentioned that there's a difference between intellectual forgiveness and emotional forgiveness. Intellectual forgiveness is choosing to forgive. It's a step in the process, but only the first step. It can occur quickly, by simply saying, for example, "I choose to forgive my mom for favoring my sister over me."

Emotional forgiveness on the other hand is actually doing the hard work of dealing directly with the person and what he or she did to you. This deep, complete forgiveness takes time and effort. You must say, "I will tell my mom in a letter exactly how she favored my sister. I will give specific examples and relive the pain of those events. I will tell Mom what her actions did to me and my view of myself, and how this rejection has harmed all my close relationships. I couldn't tell her these things as a child, but I can as an adult."

Once you have covered in your letter—in detail—how your mom harmed you and your feelings about her behavior, then you can write: "Mom, I forgive you for all the things you did to cause me pain." Writing down the wrongs done to you and your forgiveness of those wrongs will help you to clean out all your pain and fully release those who hurt you from any debt, real or perceived, owed you.

Part C: The transfer to your relationship
In the third part of each letter address your partner directly and describe how the pain and learned behaviors of your experience with the person in your past are now transferring to your partner. Be as specific as possible. Your work in Part A will help illuminate these points of transfer. You might say:

> &■ "My mom was the queen of denial. That's why I keep my real emotions hidden from you and pretend everything's fine."

ॐ "Just as I learned to do with my dad, I rant and rave at you when I'm angry."

ॐ "The only way to please my ex and get at least some acceptance and love was to kill myself doing all the chores and housework. So that's why I'm doing the same thing in our relationship."

ॐ "Because my dad disappointed me so many times, I built a wall around me to keep from getting hurt again."

I can't overstate the power of seeing clearly how you are repeating in your present relationship destructive patterns from past relationships. When you clean out your emotional pain connected to those individuals in the past and identify how you are transferring that pain now, you can finally stop making the same old mistakes with your partner.

These letters don't have to be long or filled with a mountain of details. Just hit the main points with honesty and openness, and that will get the job done.

Here is a brief, bare-bones sample letter, using fictionalized names, to show you how it's done:

Dear Dad,

You were a good provider and spent time with me doing sports. You didn't cheat on Mom, didn't abuse alcohol or drugs, and treated Mom pretty well. But you made mistakes that hurt me and shaped me as a man.

I need to be honest with you so I can heal and stop transferring my pain to my lady.

Number one, you were so critical of me. I couldn't do anything good enough for you: my grades, my chores, my attitude, my sports, my jobs, my girlfriends. You'd tell me you were trying to push me to excel, but guess what? You were wrong.

Your constant criticism demotivated me. I gave up because it wasn't worth the effort. I knew I couldn't please you. You shredded my self-esteem, Dad. I was hurt, humiliated, incredibly frustrated, and angry. Since I couldn't express my anger to you, I stuffed it. I wouldn't give you the satisfaction of seeing my anger.

Number two, you made Mom do everything around the home. When you got home, your day was over. She cooked, cleaned, did homework with us, got us to bed, and paid the bills. I learned from you that all these jobs are women's work.

Dad, I need to forgive you for those hurtful actions. I have been angry and hurt long enough. With God's help I want to let it all go. I forgive you for what you did wrong.

Betty,

I think we now know how I've transferred my dad's hurtful actions and poor teaching to you and our relationship, but I want to spell it out. First, I can't take any criticism from you, even on small things. Even when you're nice about it and only want our relationship to get better, I get defensive and angry. I blow up, say mean things, and then clam up.

I need to remember that you're not my father. His criticism was negative and just hurt me. When you bring up an issue, it's because you care about me and want the best for us.

Also I've been lazy at home, just like my dad. You do far too much, and I do far too little. No excuses. I know my laziness has made you feel unloved and unappreciated, not to mention tired and resentful. I want to be a team player and do my fair share of the chores and parenting.

Love, Frank

Step 2: Read the letters.

I want you to finish writing your letters in five to six days. This is an intense and difficult assignment, so you'll need to carve out at least three to four hours total to write. It's also best not to do them all in one sitting; that would take too much time and be too emotionally demanding. Chip away at the letters, writing for a half hour at a sitting. Many of my clients write Part A, take a break for several hours or a day to process and pray, and then return to complete Parts B and C.

It would be ideal for you to be done by a Friday. Then sit down on Friday evening and begin to read your letters out loud to each other.

I recommend you schedule three separate reading times: one on Friday, one on Saturday, and one on Sunday. You'll each read one letter per reading time. Each session will probably last thirty to forty-five minutes. If you have each written three letters (Mom, Dad, and ex-spouse, for example), this schedule will get you through all the readings by day's end on Sunday.

Most of my clients end up writing five to seven letters. I am using three letters only to show you how the process works over the course of one week. If you have more than three letters to write—and you probably will—you'll need at least two weeks to write and read them.

You may adjust this time frame if needed. If you finish your letters before Friday, you can start your reading sessions early. If it takes you longer than anticipated to finish writing, you may delay your reading sessions. If some of your letters contain a deep level of pain and trauma, it will take longer to write them. Take all the time you need.

Here's how a reading session works. You sit down in a private, quiet place. It could be the place you use for your Couple Talk Times. There should be no kids present, of course, and no one within hearing distance. No pets. No distractions. No phones. No interruptions. Pray briefly, out loud, that God will use these painful letters to help you eliminate any toxic pain transfer that is at work in your relationship.

I recommend that you first read the letters you have written to your parents, since your pain and issues in relationships began with them. Also the process works best if the two letters you read per session are letters you both have written to the same persons. For example, you could follow this format:

- First session: Both of you read your mom letters.

- Second session: Both of you read your dad letters.

- Third session: Both of you read your ex letters.

The man reads his letter first in each session. He reads his entire letter while his partner listens attentively and in silence. This is about *his* experiences and feelings only. When he is done, she makes comments that are positive, supportive, and encouraging. Briefly, in five minutes or less, she thanks him for writing the letter and tells him she's going to work to understand what he went through in this past relationship. She may comment on painful memories he related that she wasn't aware of, or she may mention some transfer points he described that she found especially interesting.

After making positive and empathic responses to his letter, the woman reads her letter. The process is now reversed, with the man listening in silence, concentrating on understanding what she is saying. He then makes positive and empathic responses in return.

Follow this same procedure in each reading session until all the letters are read and you've offered encouraging, understanding words to each other about them.

Step 3: Have follow-up talks.

After you finish reading your letters to each other, exchange them. Your next assignment is to have three follow-up talks about the letters.

Before these follow-up talks, take time to read your partner's letters several times in a sincere effort to better understand his or her past-pain and transfer issues. As you read and reread your partner's letters, pick out painful memories and learned negative behaviors he or she developed from those past painful experiences that you want to discuss further. Jot down comments and questions that occur to you as well.

Take fifteen to twenty minutes at your regularly scheduled Couple Talk Times to have these follow-up talks. Pray briefly before each one, asking God to bless your efforts to recognize and begin the process of eliminating transfer from past relationships.

The man goes first and talks about his letters (venting any still-present emotional pain, expressing words of forgiveness, and identifying points of transfer of which he is guilty). Then he asks the woman to bring up any of the memories and transfer matters from his letters she wants to discuss.

You will have strong emotional responses to certain parts of your partner's letters. These sections will make you feel intense empathy for him. Let him know, "I am so sorry you were humiliated by that football coach."

Certain sections of his letters will trigger your own painful memories. Share these with him. Say, for instance, "The way your mom rejected you at the spelling bee reminds me of the time my dad rejected me at my dance class."

Tell him how you see his pain influencing his life and your relationship. For instance, "Your mom's rejection has caused you to lack confidence in your own abilities and to distrust me and refuse to open up to me for fear that I will reject you."

When all of one partner's letters have been talked through, move on to the other partner's letters.

In these follow-up talks, the support, understanding, acceptance, and empathy that each of you needs truly get reinforced. You are talking on a deeply personal and vulnerable level, and you will create intimate connections. You will heal together and wipe out negative transfer to your relationship.

Here's a final, important point. If you have serious, traumatic past pain—such as physical, psychological, or sexual abuse; rape; or an abortion—you'll need more than these weeks to heal and eliminate harmful transfer to your partner. It may take six months or longer. Please take the time necessary to work through your pain. After you complete the work in this book, find a Christian professional therapist, and with your partner as your chief supporter, face your pain and heal from it. Typically you'll do a combination of individual and couples therapy.

What Will Block Us?

- How difficult will this letter-writing assignment be for you? Why?

- What would be your reasons for refusing to do it?

- Do these reasons for staying in your pain and its effects on your relationship outweigh the benefits of writing letters, reading them, and doing the follow-up talks?

- Can you be this vulnerable with your partner?

- Do you feel ready to write your letters? If not, why?

- Do you need to do some individual therapy dealing with your past pain before writing your letters?

LET'S PRACTICE

Time to dive into the deep end of the pool! Take the next five or six days to write your letters. Then spend three days reading your letters to each other. Finally, use three of your Couple Talk Times to do your follow-up talks.

Couples who complete this assignment send a strong message to each other that they are "all in." They truly love each other and are committed to making their relationship the best and most intimate it can be.

How Did We Do?

• What was the toughest part of carrying out the three action steps in this chapter? Why?

• How do you feel you did at providing empathy, understanding, and support for your partner? Ask your partner how he or she feels you did in these areas.

• Do you feel closer to your partner after completing the three action steps?

• If you realize your past pain is deep and you need therapy to heal, will you call a Christian therapist?

ESSENTIAL AREA 5

WE NEED TO TALK
ABOUT OUR POSITIVITY

CHAPTER 9

PUCKER UP, PLAY, AND PURSUE

*Y*OU SURVIVED THE last two chapters—well done! You deserve a reward. (Well, in addition to the benefits you're already receiving from doing the hard work included in those chapters).

Your reward is a much more lighthearted, fun chapter. You're welcome.

THE WOOING OF THE CLARKE GIRLS

Emily, Leeann, and Nancy are our three wonderful daughters. All three are married: Emily to Chaz, Leeann to Andrew, and Nancy to Phil. All three husbands are outstanding young men.

No father thinks any guy is worthy of his daughters, but these men passed my rigorous inspection with flying colors. Plus my daughters fell madly in love with them, so what was I going to do?

Sandy and I watched with great interest and, frankly, entertainment as these suitors courted our daughters. Each of them mounted an impressive campaign of romantic pursuit. When one of them would take some amazing action to show his love, Sandy would say, "He's good. He's very, very good."

Here's a snapshot of some of the positive, caring,

romantic, pre-engagement behaviors of these three knights in shining armor.

Chaz

- Once they were a couple, Chaz gave Emily a special gift on their one-month anniversary: flowers, a card, and chocolates. He continued to demonstrate his affection this way every month for months. I mean, who does that? A man in love.

- Emily likes plays, so Chaz took her to plays. Trust me, he's not a play-going man. But they went to a number of plays at community playhouses. Emily was happy, and that's all that mattered to Chaz.

- Emily loves sappy, tear-jerking movies. Chaz, being a normal man, doesn't. But for Emily he sat through many chick movies, including *A Walk to Remember*, which is perhaps the most depressing movie ever made—a teenage girl is dying of cancer, and she and her boyfriend go through the hideous, drawn-out ordeal together. Chaz sat and suffered through it. That's an act of true love and devotion.

Andrew

- Andrew helped Leeann when her old car broke down several times. She called her car the Bullet because it was red and sporty. It should have been called the Dud the last few

years she had it. It was literally falling apart.
It should have been pushed over a cliff, but
we don't have any cliffs in Florida. When it
would break down, she'd call Andrew, and
he'd come running to help her. He can fix
anything, so he'd fix it. I joked to him that
Leeann was using her crummy car to test his
love. He passed.

&v Andrew drove an hour one way every Sunday
to attend Leeann's church. She loved her
church and her pastor, and she had many
friends there. Andrew went to the church
to please Leeann—and believe me, she was
pleased.

&v For several months during their dating days,
Leeann had trouble sleeping. She'd wake up
in the middle of the night feeling anxious
and stressed. Andrew told her, "Call me every
time you can't sleep. I don't care what time it
is. We'll talk it out." Leeann called him many
times, and he was patient and kind. On those
nights there were two persons who couldn't
sleep. But Andrew didn't care because his
sweetheart needed him.

Phil

&v Our third daughter, Nancy, is an excellent
tennis player. She played on her high school
team. Phil didn't play tennis. Phil didn't even
own a tennis racquet. But when Nancy asked
him to play tennis, he said yes. He talked

some smack before their first game, but he was wiped off the court by his feisty, tennis-playing girlfriend. Phil took it like a man. He didn't love tennis. He loved Nancy.

≈ Nancy was into swing dancing, which, of course, is every man's dream activity. Well, I'm sure there are men who love it. But Phil isn't one of them. Phil is a terrific musician and worship leader, but he is not a dancer. Even so, did he go swing dancing with Nancy? Sure he did. Love means you do things your partner wants to do.

≈ Phil wrote Nancy an original song and sang it to her while playing his guitar. That was a mind-blower! Talk about world-class romantic pursuit. When I heard about the performance, I said to Sandy, "You just have to marry a guy like that. If she doesn't marry him, I will."

As you can see, there was a tremendous amount of positivity in these three courting couples. Not an ounce of negativity. And the positive flow went both ways. The girls did many positive, loving things for their guys too.

Just about every couple experiences extreme positivity during the courtship phase. If that positivity isn't there, something is seriously wrong, and you ought to break up and move on. When you're falling in love, everything's great. Everything's wonderful. It should be!

HERE COME THE NEGATIVES

Unfortunately your 24/7 positivity doesn't last. When your marriage is about a year and a half old—really, when you start living together—the negatives begin.

Annoying habits (not yours, of course!). Male-female differences. In-law issues (not your parents, of course!). Spending habits. Communication problems. Needs not being met. The hectic pace of life. Jobs. The many compromises you have to make in many areas. Different sleep-wake cycles. Distribution of household chores. Does this sound familiar?

And then you go and have a baby! What were you thinking? Now your precious child takes over your lives, and the stress level in all of the above areas goes way up. Your child is not a negative, of course, but his or her presence certainly makes your relationship more difficult. You still love each other. No one's talking about breaking up. But the negatives are starting to outnumber the positives.

If that trend continues, your relationship is in trouble. Real trouble. Pretty soon all you'll have is negatives, and you'll be allowing your relationship to die.

In a love relationship the positives must always outweigh the negatives. Always. And the ratio shouldn't even be close. Maintaining a high number of positives keeps you in love and allows you to deal successfully with the inevitable negatives.

THIS IS MISSION CRITICAL

I want you to understand something important. When you're in the infatuation/courtship phase, your passionate feelings of love drive your positive behaviors. Because you're madly in love, you do positive and caring things for your partner. Feelings come first, and behavior follows.

Once the infatuation phase is over and the negatives begin to creep in, you're in a whole different ball game. From now on behavior will come first, and feelings will follow. You will have to carry out positive and loving actions in order to generate in-love, passionate feelings. In other words, *do* first, and the feelings will follow. Don't wait for the feelings to show up before acting.

That's my job in this chapter: to help you to get back on track, and stay on track, in the "positives drive feelings" department. When you keep your positives high, you keep your feelings of love and passion high.

The great news is the small loving actions are what make the difference. Big, expensive, romantic events are wonderful, but they're too infrequent to generate lasting love. The beach vacations, the cruises, and the concerts will not keep your love hot, exciting, and expanding. The daily and weekly positive behaviors will.

How Are We Doing?

- Look back at your dating days or the first year or so of your relationship. How did you feel about each other? How powerful and vibrant was your love?

- During this pre-living-together phase, what positive things did you do for each other?

- What negatives began to pop up in your relationship? (Review the list of negatives included earlier in this chapter if that helps jog your memory.)

- What are the main negatives right now in your relationship? How are these negatives affecting your love for your partner?

- What positive behaviors have you reduced in number or dropped entirely?

HERE'S WHAT WE CAN DO

Here are three small, simple behaviors that will inject a regular flow of positivity into your relationship.

Pucker up, baby!

In my professional and personal opinion kissing is a big deal in the life of a couple. Every kiss is an intense, intimate, romantic event. Or at least it should be. As the kisser you want your *every kiss* to communicate your love and passion for the kissee: "I deeply love you. I want you. I need you. I'm crazy about you."

Most couples, however, lose the ability to kiss in this "va-va-voom, oh baby" way after they've been married a while. As their powerful feelings of love fade, so does their kissing.

They give little pecks: two dried-out, closed sets of lips touching for a millisecond. Really? This is kissing? Or they make the sound of kissing without really kissing; standing only ten feet apart, each partner makes a smooching sound. Really? Or they do the dreaded *cheek* kiss—a gentle whisper of a kiss a good two inches from where the real kiss is supposed to land. Really?

If you're kissing your mother, your aunt, an old lady at church, or a close friend, these "kisses" are fine. But they are not fine with your sweetheart! They are insulting and wrong and anemic and a clear indication that your passion has pooped out.

You know how to kiss each other. You used to do it all the time when you were first married. It's time to crank up the real kissing: open-mouthed, long, lingering, heartfelt smackers! Hold each kiss for ten seconds, and saliva— the golden nectar of great kisses—will be generated. Once you have saliva, you can start sliding your lips around and...well, you know what I mean.

Each kiss should also include sensual body contact— arms around each other, hands on your spouse's face, and a full-body hug. Now, that's a kiss!

And one more thing. Will one kiss like this be enough? If you said no, give yourself a prize. Of course one great kiss isn't enough! Two or three great kisses create real feelings of love and passion.

Kiss like this when you part in the morning. Do it again when you come back together in the evening. Kiss every single time one of you leaves the house for whatever reason. Kiss passionately after your Couple Talk Times. Kiss like you mean it after watching a favorite television show or movie. Kiss in this way before going to sleep at night.

Get your kissing back on track, and you'll get your passion back on track.

Play with me, baby!

Go out regularly on fun, playful dates. I strongly recommend once a week. No kids; they're driving you crazy, and you have to get away from them. No pets. No family. Just the two of you.

Don't do the same old boring routine of dinner and a movie. Be creative! Doing activities you did back when you were first dating will bring back great, happy memories and romantic feelings.

Also try new, out-of-the-box ideas. You don't have to spend a lot of money; the best dates are cheap. To keep your dates fresh and to make sure both your needs are met, take turns planning your dates. This week the man gets to plan the date. Next week the woman gets to take a turn.

The list of possible activities is almost endless. Look for activities that allow you to interact and communicate. Again, what you do isn't as important as being together and having fun. Remember, you're going out to play!

Pursue me, baby!

Romantic pursuit is doing what your partner enjoys doing. It's not about you; it's about your partner and making him or her happy. Chaz, Andrew, and Phil made our girls happy by doing things they knew the girls would enjoy. The girls then turned around and made the guys happy by doing what the guys wanted to do. That's how pursuit works!

Find out—by observing and asking—what your partner likes to do. Then follow through and do that activity. It's that simple. At least once a week have some togetherness time doing an activity your partner enjoys.

My Sandy loves watching remodeling shows on television. It's true—somebody created an entire channel of these shows. If I could find him, I'd give him a beating. Or I'd demolish his home and say, "It's time to remodel, don't you think?"

I hate those shows. I'm not handy. I like my home just the way it is. And I'm super cheap and don't want to spend huge amounts of money.

To pursue my wife though, I watch at least one of these shows each week with her. I sit there, try not to make any snarky comments (that's tough!), and listen to Sandy comment on all the remodeling and what she'd like to do to an already perfect home. If that isn't loving pursuit, I don't know what is.

I should receive the Nobel Prize for Romantic Pursuit!

Alternatively, Sandy pursues me by touching me. I love to be touched by my bride, and I'm not talking about sex. Don't get me wrong—I want sex too. But I'm talking about nonsexual, affectionate touching, such as a scalp massage, foot massage, or neck message.

In fact, I'm getting excited just writing this. When Sandy gives me a fifteen-minute scalp, foot, or neck massage, I feel loved. I feel happy. I feel close to her. (The experience is even better if I don't have to beg for it.)

Now I've gotten the impression that Sandy isn't wild about giving me these massages. It's not her thing. I don't know why—after all, it's a privilege to touch my body! But she does it to pursue me and to make me feel happy and loved.

There is no true romance without pursuit. It takes effort. It pushes you outside your comfort zone. But when you pursue your partner, you create fun, romance, passion, and a deeper love for each other.

What Will Block Us?

- Talk about the state of your kissing and how you both feel about it. How often do you kiss passionately? What will be difficult about giving real kisses every day?

- Do you have excuses for not going out on a date every week? Talk about this. Is it money, time, difficulty finding a babysitter, an inability to think of fun things to do? Or is it that you feel awkward being together, have lost the joy you once knew in being together, or maybe are out of practice?

- Why don't you do activities that you know your partner would enjoy? Is it selfishness? Is it payback for your partner hurting you in some way? Is it happening because you have begun to live separate lives and to focus on your own activities?

LET'S PRACTICE

OK, you know what to do this week:

1. Kiss in a passionate way multiple times a day.

2. Go out on a fun, romantic date.

3. Do an activity that your partner enjoys.

And here's a quick message for those of you whose relationship is in bad shape: for you these positive behaviors will be very difficult to carry out; the good feelings aren't there. But I want you to force yourselves to do them. Do it for God and for your spouse. It will take time, but eventually these positive *actions* will create loving *feelings*.

Don't give up. Keep on doing them until the feelings come.

How Did We Do?

- What was the best part for you this week? Was it the kissing, the date, or the pursuit activities?

- Tell your partner how these positive behaviors affected your feelings of love and passion.

- What was the most difficult positive action for you to do? Why?

- Are you willing to commit to continuing these three positive behaviors in your relationship? What could potentially stop you from doing them?

ESSENTIAL AREA 6

WE NEED TO TALK ABOUT OUR NEEDS

CHAPTER 10

WE REALLY DO
NEED EACH OTHER

I LOVE MY BEAUTIFUL, smart, capable, fun wife, Sandy. My sleep apnea odyssey proves it. Those who suffer from this hideous disorder and its equally hideous "treatment" know exactly what I'm talking about. And if you don't know about the horrors of sleep apnea, you're about to find out.

(Warning: Do not read this story on a full stomach or at night when you're all alone.)

It all started one awful morning at breakfast when Sandy said, "You've been snoring loudly for the past two weeks. And not just snoring. Two or three times a night, you rip off massive snorts."

She continued, "At first, I thought these were shotgun blasts or a car backfiring. Then I realized it was you. I can't sleep. I've done some research, and I think you have sleep apnea"—that's an intermittent cessation of breathing while sleeping—"and I want you to get checked out by a sleep doctor."

And so my nightmare began.

My mom, Kathy Clarke, is an RN who knows every doctor in town personally, and she found me a sleep doctor. After a five-minute evaluation, I was—what a shocker!—diagnosed with sleep apnea. Every sucker—I mean, person—who sees a sleep doctor will be diagnosed with sleep apnea. That's my theory. You may go in with a hemorrhoid condition, but you will come out with sleep apnea.

The next step on my incredible sleep apnea journey was the Sleep Center. Don't be fooled by the name. Sleep has absolutely nothing to do with these centers. I recommended to the staff that they change the name to the No One Sleeps Here Center. They didn't seem to appreciate my attempt at humor.

At the Sleep Center a sleep technician spent forty-five minutes attaching two thousand wires to almost every part of my body. I was rolled onto my back, weighed down by all the wires, and lying in a small bed in a strange little room that looked suspiciously like a prison cell. The technician—with a straight face—said, "As you sleep tonight, we will be monitoring a number of your vital signs so we can get a clear picture of the level and activity of your sleep apnea. Oh, and we will be watching you by video all night."

I replied, "You can't be serious. You think there's a remote chance I will sleep in this torture chamber? Look, I'll give you a hundred bucks if you'll let me go and report that I don't have sleep apnea."

The technician gave me no response other than a patronizing smile.

The result of my sleepless night at the No One Sleeps Here Center was the shocking confirmation of my sleep apnea diagnosis.

It was the beginning of a yearlong search for the right mask. No, not like the masks of the Lone Ranger or Batman. You see, every night of your miserable life, you have to strap on a mask that is connected to a CPAP, or continuous positive airway pressure, machine via a tube. The machine forces air through the tube, into the mask, and into your mouth and nose. Brilliant scientists and manufacturers of sleep apnea equipment have concluded that having compressed air forced into your face will help you have a peaceful night's sleep.

The good news is the mask and the tubing and the rushing air totally eliminate snoring and snorting. The bad news is that's because you're not sleeping!

I finally found the right mask and can actually sleep at night. But make no mistake. I still hate it. I do it for Sandy because I love her and want to meet her needs. And yes, I want credit for my enormous sacrifice.

The truth is Sandy has done many, many wonderful things for me over the years too. As I pursued my graduate studies in biblical studies and clinical psychology, I dragged her to Dallas, Texas; Portland, Oregon; Mount Gretna, Pennsylvania; and finally Tampa, Florida. She worked all those years so I could go to school and so we could eat. She's been a tremendous wife and a terrific mom to our kids. She's been a loving and supportive partner all along. Now we work together at my ministry in Tampa.

I could fill a book—a library—with all she's done to meet my needs.

Frankly, the least I can do for her is wear an uncomfortable mask to bed every night that pumps air into my face so I don't snore or snort (or stop breathing).

IF YOU LOVE ME, YOU'LL MEET MY NEEDS

You and your partner have core needs. These needs require both of you to practice specific behaviors that make each of you feel loved. These needs are normal, innate, and God-given. They are personality based, an essential part of who you are, and they don't change over your lifetime.

Here is a list of core needs my clients have expressed over the years:

- "Touch me physically."

- "Make love to me."

- "Do helpful things for me."

- "Verbally romance me."

- "Take actions to romance me."

- "Verbally respect me."

- "Spend private, personal time with me."

- "Lead me."

- "Have deeper conversations with me."

- "Laugh with me."

- "Connect spiritually with me."

To feel truly loved, you must have your core needs met on a regular basis. And they can be met only by your significant other. (It must be stated here that as individuals we have needs in our lives that only God can meet. Trusting in Him to meet those needs is the key to lifelong happiness as we discussed in chapters 4 and 5 under the essential area of spiritual intimacy.)

But here's the catch. It will be very difficult for you to meet each other's core needs. It will not come naturally. In fact, meeting your partner's core needs will be your area of greatest weakness. Doesn't seem fair, does it? Well, who said love is fair? Love is hard.

Let me give you some examples.

not one of them is alone.
Your lips are like a scarlet ribbon;
    your mouth is lovely.
Your temples behind your veil
    are like the halves of a pomegranate.
Your neck is like the tower of David,
    built with courses of stone;
on it hang a thousand shields,
    all of them shields of warriors.
Your breasts are like two fawns,
    like twin fawns of a gazelle
    that browse among the lilies.
Until the day breaks
    and the shadows flee,
I will go to the mountain of myrrh
    and to the hill of incense.
You are altogether beautiful, my darling;
    there is no flaw in you.

Solomon is obviously praising her physical body here, but in several of these verses he uses a physical description to convey praise of her character and personality as well.

- *Your eyes behind your veil are doves* means her character is pure, morally upright, and innocent.

- *Your neck is like the tower of David* means she is a woman of integrity, elegance, and strength.

- *You are altogether beautiful* means she is perfect physically and as a person.

As I mentioned in the last chapter, one of my core needs is touch. To feel loved by my wife, I need her to touch me in affectionate ways every day. Sex is great, but I don't need that every day. It could be a scalp massage. A neck massage. A foot massage. Rubbing my hand as we watch television. Now, that's what I'm talking about! These touches, which only Sandy can do for me, send me to the moon—the love moon.

These daily touches are not easy for Sandy to do though. She is a wonderful and loving wife, but she is not a naturally physically affectionate person, at least not at the level I need. Yet she generously indulges me with affectionate touch because she knows I need it to feel loved by her.

On the other hand, one of Sandy's core needs is help with household chores. To feel loved by me, she needs to see me doing jobs around the house every day. She is a doer and expresses her love for others by doing things for them, so it makes sense that she would feel loved when I do things for her. This means cleaning up after dinner. Loading and unloading the dishwasher. Taking out the trash. Mowing the lawn. Keeping the pool clean. Doing a load of laundry. Vacuuming. Paying the bills. When I do jobs like these every day, I send Sandy to *her* love moon.

Guess what one of my weaknesses is? Doing household chores! Wouldn't you know it? My mom did just about everything for me when I was growing up, so I never got into chores. I didn't have to. But since I want Sandy to feel loved by me, I have to suck it up every day and do my chores.

My CPAP story at the beginning of this chapter reveals another one of Sandy's core needs: a quiet, peaceful bedroom that will give her a restful night's sleep. After some resistance I took dramatic steps to meet this core need.

How Are We Doing?

- Tell your partner your top three core needs.

- Of these three, state which one is most important to you and why.

- Ask your partner how you are doing meeting his or her core needs.

- If meeting one of your partner's core needs is difficult for you, discuss why.

HERE'S WHAT WE CAN DO

You have many individual core needs, but I'm going to zero in on two that are common to every couple. These needs are illustrated in the relationship of King Solomon and Shulamith, the two lovers in the book of Song of Solomon in the Bible.

Solomon and Shulamith (also known as the Shulamite woman) have an amazing love characterized by closeness and passion. How do they do it? One of their secrets is that each one has a core need that the other meets every day through verbal communication.

"Am I beautiful to you today?"

Shulamith's core need is to be *verbally romanced*. Every woman in a relationship has this need. Every day your woman is asking the same question: "Am I beautiful to you today?" She needs to know today that you find her desirable and attractive. And she needs to know again tomorrow and the next day and the day after that…

In Song of Solomon 1:15–2:3, we see Shulamith's need

for Solomon's praise. He praises her, she feels loved and romanced, and she praises him right back. In the second part of Song of Solomon 2:3, she says, "His fruit is sweet to my taste." By *fruit* she means the romantic things he verbalizes to her.

Furthermore, she needs to know she is not just physically beautiful, but beautiful as a person.

Solomon is smart enough (see 1 Kings 4:29) to know that a woman has to know she is beautiful. However, simply walking up to her and saying, "You are beautiful," isn't enough. It's a good start—don't get me wrong—but it's not enough to meet her core need of being verbally romanced.

Have you ever said to your woman, "I love you," and then been hit with the immediate response, "Why?" (A pause of more than a nanosecond here is not a good idea.) A woman requires the details. The explanation. The why. The story of her beauty.

It's your job as her man to tell her that story every day.

Practically every time he is in her presence, Solomon tells Shulamith how beautiful she is. She does not have to prompt him. He spontaneously tells her. In Song of Solomon 4:1–7, Solomon describes in detail Shulamith's beauty in three areas: her body and its attributes, her character, and her personality traits:

> How beautiful you are, my darling!
>> Oh, how beautiful!
>> Your eyes behind your veil are doves.
> Your hair is like a flock of goats
>> descending from the hills of Gilead.
> Your teeth are like a flock of sheep just shorn,
>> coming up from the washing.
> Each has its twin;

To Solomon, Shulamith is the most beautiful woman in the world in every way, outside and inside, and he convinces her of this truth daily.

"Am I impressive to you today?"

Solomon's core need, on the other hand, is to be *verbally respected*. Again, every man in a relationship has this need. Every day your man is asking the same question: "Am I impressive to you today?" He needs to know that today— and every day—you find him an impressive man worthy of your respect and admiration.

Do you think *admiration* is going too far? Believe me, it's not. If you, ma'am, don't make your admiration of your man crystal clear every day, he will not feel loved by you. He won't feel close to you. He will lose confidence in himself and in your relationship.

But when he feels admired by you, his core need of respect is met. He will automatically feel loved by you, close to you, and confident in himself and in your relationship.

I cannot overstate the importance of verbal respect— using actual words—in the life of your man. He certainly likes respect from others, but he *needs* it from you. The admiration Sandy offers me means infinitely more than the admiration offered me by anyone else.

Shulamith has the power to make Solomon feel impressive, and she does that by praising him in three areas: his character, his career, and his body. Song of Solomon 5:10-16, is just one passage where she compliments Solomon in these three areas:

> My beloved is radiant and ruddy,
>   outstanding among ten thousand.
> His head is purest gold;

his hair is wavy
and black as a raven.
His eyes are like doves
by the water streams,
washed in milk,
mounted like jewels,
His cheeks are like beds of spice
yielding perfume.
His lips are like lilies
dripping with myrrh.
His arms are rods of gold
set with topaz.
His body is like polished ivory
decorated with lapis lazuli.
His legs are pillars of marble
set on bases of pure gold.
His appearance is like Lebanon,
choice as its cedars.
His mouth is sweetness itself;
he is altogether lovely.
This is my beloved, this is my friend,
daughters of Jerusalem.

In this passage Shulamith is praising Solomon's physical attractiveness. But just as Solomon did in the passage above, she is praising his other qualities as well—in this case, his character and his career.

> *Outstanding among ten thousand* means he is the most impressive man she knows.

> *His eyes are like doves* means he is a gentle, sensitive, loving man.

&❧ *His lips are like lilies dripping with myrrh*
means he is a passionate, romantic man.

&❧ *His legs are pillars of marble* means his character is strong and he can protect her and
lead her.

Keep in mind, Solomon is the king, yet he still needs the
woman he loves to tell him every day what she sees in him
that inspires her feelings of respect. Learn from Shulamith's
example. She knows that a man has to hear in detail how
she is impressed by him. And he needs to hear it every day.
Just as a woman doubts her beauty, a man doubts his value
in her estimation.

What Will Block Us?

- Man, what will be hard for you about verbally
  romancing your woman?

- Woman, what will be hard for you about
  verbally respecting your man?

- Did you see your parents meet these two
  core needs in each other's life?

- What will stop you from meeting these core
  needs for each other?

LET'S PRACTICE

Sit down by yourself in a private place and write down
seven compliments that will meet your partner's core need
of *verbal romance* (for her) or *verbal respect* (for him).

If you're the man, your compliments will be focused on your woman's (1) body, (2) character, and (3) personality traits. Write at least two compliments in each category. Here's a sample list:

- ❧ "Your eyes are stunning."

- ❧ "You have the most gorgeous legs in the world."

- ❧ "You are very compassionate to those in need."

- ❧ "Your love for Jesus is deep."

- ❧ "I love your quirky sense of humor."

- ❧ "I love how you make really good friends."

- ❧ "When you start a job, you finish it."

If you're the woman, your seven compliments will be focused on your man's (1) character, (2) career, and (3) body. Again, write down at least two compliments in each category. Here's a sample list:

- ❧ "You are a man of integrity."

- ❧ "You are a very loyal person."

- ❧ "I'm proud of the work you do at your job."

- ❧ "What you do at work serves an important purpose."

- ❧ "I admire how you handled that work project."

- ❧ "Your mustache is beyond cool."

- ❧ "Your biceps are pretty amazing."

When your list is finished, lay one compliment per day on your partner. Be specific, and be sincere. Saying it in person is best, but if you can't see each other, a phone call or text will work.

How Did We Do?

- Was it hard for you to think of compliments?

- Was it hard to deliver the compliments?

- How did it feel to hear the compliments your partner offered you?

- Which compliments meant the most to you? Why?

- If you have another core need that is important to you besides verbal romance or verbal respect, identify it and tell your partner exactly how to meet it.

HOW TO MEET NEEDS EVERY DAY

*A*s we discussed in the last chapter, in a serious love relationship each partner has core needs. These are personality-based, permanent-over-a-lifetime needs that when met, make someone feel deeply loved.

Each partner also has *secondary needs*. These are lower-level, maintenance needs that when met, reduce stress, create teamwork, and keep the relationship running smoothly. Meeting these needs prepares each of you to meet your partner's core needs.

Here are some examples of a partner's secondary needs:

- Make my coffee in the morning.
- Make the kids' lunches in the morning.
- Make the bed in the morning.
- Go to the grocery store and get these items.
- Do a load of laundry, fold it, and put it away.
- Mow the lawn.
- Help the kids with their homework.
- Call the plumber and get an appointment.

When your list is finished, lay one compliment per day on your partner. Be specific, and be sincere. Saying it in person is best, but if you can't see each other, a phone call or text will work.

How Did We Do?

- Was it hard for you to think of compliments?

- Was it hard to deliver the compliments?

- How did it feel to hear the compliments your partner offered you?

- Which compliments meant the most to you? Why?

- If you have another core need that is important to you besides verbal romance or verbal respect, identify it and tell your partner exactly how to meet it.

HOW TO MEET
NEEDS EVERY DAY

*A*s we discussed in the last chapter, in a serious love relationship each partner has core needs. These are personality-based, permanent-over-a-lifetime needs that when met, make someone feel deeply loved.

Each partner also has *secondary needs*. These are lower-level, maintenance needs that when met, reduce stress, create teamwork, and keep the relationship running smoothly. Meeting these needs prepares each of you to meet your partner's core needs.

Here are some examples of a partner's secondary needs:

- Make my coffee in the morning.

- Make the kids' lunches in the morning.

- Make the bed in the morning.

- Go to the grocery store and get these items.

- Do a load of laundry, fold it, and put it away.

- Mow the lawn.

- Help the kids with their homework.

- Call the plumber and get an appointment.

As I mentioned in the last chapter, one of my core needs is touch. To feel loved by my wife, I need her to touch me in affectionate ways every day. Sex is great, but I don't need that every day. It could be a scalp massage. A neck massage. A foot massage. Rubbing my hand as we watch television. Now, that's what I'm talking about! These touches, which only Sandy can do for me, send me to the moon—the love moon.

These daily touches are not easy for Sandy to do though. She is a wonderful and loving wife, but she is not a naturally physically affectionate person, at least not at the level I need. Yet she generously indulges me with affectionate touch because she knows I need it to feel loved by her.

On the other hand, one of Sandy's core needs is help with household chores. To feel loved by me, she needs to see me doing jobs around the house every day. She is a doer and expresses her love for others by doing things for them, so it makes sense that she would feel loved when I do things for her. This means cleaning up after dinner. Loading and unloading the dishwasher. Taking out the trash. Mowing the lawn. Keeping the pool clean. Doing a load of laundry. Vacuuming. Paying the bills. When I do jobs like these every day, I send Sandy to *her* love moon.

Guess what one of my weaknesses is? Doing household chores! Wouldn't you know it? My mom did just about everything for me when I was growing up, so I never got into chores. I didn't have to. But since I want Sandy to feel loved by me, I have to suck it up every day and do my chores.

My CPAP story at the beginning of this chapter reveals another one of Sandy's core needs: a quiet, peaceful bedroom that will give her a restful night's sleep. After some resistance I took dramatic steps to meet this core need.

How Are We Doing?

- Tell your partner your top three core needs.

- Of these three, state which one is most important to you and why.

- Ask your partner how you are doing meeting his or her core needs.

- If meeting one of your partner's core needs is difficult for you, discuss why.

HERE'S WHAT WE CAN DO

You have many individual core needs, but I'm going to zero in on two that are common to every couple. These needs are illustrated in the relationship of King Solomon and Shulamith, the two lovers in the book of Song of Solomon in the Bible.

Solomon and Shulamith (also known as the Shulamite woman) have an amazing love characterized by closeness and passion. How do they do it? One of their secrets is that each one has a core need that the other meets every day through verbal communication.

"Am I beautiful to you today?"

Shulamith's core need is to be *verbally romanced*. Every woman in a relationship has this need. Every day your woman is asking the same question: "Am I beautiful to you today?" She needs to know today that you find her desirable and attractive. And she needs to know again tomorrow and the next day and the day after that…

In Song of Solomon 1:15–2:3, we see Shulamith's need

for Solomon's praise. He praises her, she feels loved and romanced, and she praises him right back. In the second part of Song of Solomon 2:3, she says, "His fruit is sweet to my taste." By *fruit* she means the romantic things he verbalizes to her.

Furthermore, she needs to know she is not just physically beautiful, but beautiful as a person.

Solomon is smart enough (see 1 Kings 4:29) to know that a woman has to know she is beautiful. However, simply walking up to her and saying, "You are beautiful," isn't enough. It's a good start—don't get me wrong—but it's not enough to meet her core need of being verbally romanced.

Have you ever said to your woman, "I love you," and then been hit with the immediate response, "Why?" (A pause of more than a nanosecond here is not a good idea.) A woman requires the details. The explanation. The why. The story of her beauty.

It's your job as her man to tell her that story every day.

Practically every time he is in her presence, Solomon tells Shulamith how beautiful she is. She does not have to prompt him. He spontaneously tells her. In Song of Solomon 4:1–7, Solomon describes in detail Shulamith's beauty in three areas: her body and its attributes, her character, and her personality traits:

> How beautiful you are, my darling!
>   Oh, how beautiful!
>   Your eyes behind your veil are doves.
> Your hair is like a flock of goats
>   descending from the hills of Gilead.
> Your teeth are like a flock of sheep just shorn,
>   coming up from the washing.
> Each has its twin;

not one of them is alone.
Your lips are like a scarlet ribbon;
    your mouth is lovely.
Your temples behind your veil
    are like the halves of a pomegranate.
Your neck is like the tower of David,
    built with courses of stone;
on it hang a thousand shields,
    all of them shields of warriors.
Your breasts are like two fawns,
    like twin fawns of a gazelle
    that browse among the lilies.
Until the day breaks
    and the shadows flee,
I will go to the mountain of myrrh
    and to the hill of incense.
You are altogether beautiful, my darling;
    there is no flaw in you.

Solomon is obviously praising her physical body here, but in several of these verses he uses a physical description to convey praise of her character and personality as well.

- *Your eyes behind your veil are doves* means her character is pure, morally upright, and innocent.

- *Your neck is like the tower of David* means she is a woman of integrity, elegance, and strength.

- *You are altogether beautiful* means she is perfect physically and as a person.

If you're the man, your compliments will be focused on your woman's (1) body, (2) character, and (3) personality traits. Write at least two compliments in each category. Here's a sample list:

- ❧ "Your eyes are stunning."

- ❧ "You have the most gorgeous legs in the world."

- ❧ "You are very compassionate to those in need."

- ❧ "Your love for Jesus is deep."

- ❧ "I love your quirky sense of humor."

- ❧ "I love how you make really good friends."

- ❧ "When you start a job, you finish it."

If you're the woman, your seven compliments will be focused on your man's (1) character, (2) career, and (3) body. Again, write down at least two compliments in each category. Here's a sample list:

- ❧ "You are a man of integrity."

- ❧ "You are a very loyal person."

- ❧ "I'm proud of the work you do at your job."

- ❧ "What you do at work serves an important purpose."

- ❧ "I admire how you handled that work project."

- ❧ "Your mustache is beyond cool."

- ❧ "Your biceps are pretty amazing."

• *His lips are like lilies dripping with myrrh* means he is a passionate, romantic man.

• *His legs are pillars of marble* means his character is strong and he can protect her and lead her.

Keep in mind, Solomon is the king, yet he still needs the woman he loves to tell him every day what she sees in him that inspires her feelings of respect. Learn from Shulamith's example. She knows that a man has to hear in detail how she is impressed by him. And he needs to hear it every day. Just as a woman doubts her beauty, a man doubts his value in her estimation.

What Will Block Us?

- Man, what will be hard for you about verbally romancing your woman?

- Woman, what will be hard for you about verbally respecting your man?

- Did you see your parents meet these two core needs in each other's life?

- What will stop you from meeting these core needs for each other?

LET'S PRACTICE

Sit down by yourself in a private place and write down seven compliments that will meet your partner's core need of *verbal romance* (for her) or *verbal respect* (for him).

his hair is wavy
and black as a raven.
His eyes are like doves
by the water streams,
washed in milk,
mounted like jewels,
His cheeks are like beds of spice
yielding perfume.
His lips are like lilies
dripping with myrrh.
His arms are rods of gold
set with topaz.
His body is like polished ivory
decorated with lapis lazuli.
His legs are pillars of marble
set on bases of pure gold.
His appearance is like Lebanon,
choice as its cedars.
His mouth is sweetness itself;
he is altogether lovely.
This is my beloved, this is my friend,
daughters of Jerusalem.

In this passage Shulamith is praising Solomon's physical attractiveness. But just as Solomon did in the passage above, she is praising his other qualities as well—in this case, his character and his career.

- *Outstanding among ten thousand* means he is the most impressive man she knows.

- *His eyes are like doves* means he is a gentle, sensitive, loving man.

To Solomon, Shulamith is the most beautiful woman in the world in every way, outside and inside, and he convinces her of this truth daily.

"Am I impressive to you today?"

Solomon's core need, on the other hand, is to be *verbally respected*. Again, every man in a relationship has this need. Every day your man is asking the same question: "Am I impressive to you today?" He needs to know that today—and every day—you find him an impressive man worthy of your respect and admiration.

Do you think *admiration* is going too far? Believe me, it's not. If you, ma'am, don't make your admiration of your man crystal clear every day, he will not feel loved by you. He won't feel close to you. He will lose confidence in himself and in your relationship.

But when he feels admired by you, his core need of respect is met. He will automatically feel loved by you, close to you, and confident in himself and in your relationship.

I cannot overstate the importance of verbal respect—using actual words—in the life of your man. He certainly likes respect from others, but he *needs* it from you. The admiration Sandy offers me means infinitely more than the admiration offered me by anyone else.

Shulamith has the power to make Solomon feel impressive, and she does that by praising him in three areas: his character, his career, and his body. Song of Solomon 5:10–16, is just one passage where she compliments Solomon in these three areas:

> My beloved is radiant and ruddy,
> > outstanding among ten thousand.
> His head is purest gold;

ꝥ Listen to me vent about my stressful day.

ꝥ Pick up dinner on the way home.

To keep your love strong and your intimacy flowing every day, you must meet at least 65 percent of your partner's core and secondary needs.

The majority of couples get nowhere near this 65 percent on a daily basis, but closer to 5 to 10 percent. At this low level of need meeting, the relationship soon gets into real trouble.

Now I know the main reason couples don't meet a high percentage of each other's core and secondary needs: the partners don't make their needs clear. I'd say 95 percent of men and women in romantic relationships are lousy at communicating their needs to their significant others. And when I say lousy, I mean *really* lousy.

WOMEN DON'T MAKE THEIR NEEDS CLEAR

What a woman says and what she means can be two totally different things. Have you noticed that, men?

> **She says:** I'll just be five minutes.
>
> **She means:** I'll be at least thirty minutes. Don't get upset. If you mention I was twenty-five minutes over time, we'll have a thirty-minute talk about your insensitivity, and that will make us another thirty minutes late. And it will be your fault.
>
> **She says:** Oh, don't make a big fuss over my birthday [or Mother's Day, Valentine's Day, our anniversary, etc.].

She means: You'd better make a big fuss over this day, buddy, or you'll never hear the end of it. I don't want to *appear* as though I want a big fuss, but I want a big fuss!

She says: [In response to the man asking her how she feels] Fine.

She means: I'm not fine. I'm as far from fine as I can be. I want you to say to me, "I know you're not fine, honey. Let's talk about it." If you don't, I'll be even more upset than I am now because I'll know you don't care about me and my feelings.

She says: Here are all the things I have to do today. [She lists her jobs.]

She means: I need your help with all these things I have to do today. Ask me what jobs you can take off my hands. If you don't ask, I'll do all my jobs but resent you for not helping.

She says: We need to talk.

She means: *We* are not going to talk. I'll be the only one talking. I'm going to spend the next twenty minutes—or more—venting about what you did or said to me to upset me. You will listen quietly, make me believe you understand the pain you've caused, thank me for sharing so honestly, admit it's your fault, and humbly apologize ten times for your crimes against me.

Sound familiar, men? I thought so. It's impossible to figure out your woman's needs because she doesn't tell you what they are. You're supposed to know! You're supposed to grasp what she really means, when what she says is completely different from what she means.

MEN DON'T MAKE THEIR NEEDS CLEAR

But wait a minute. I want to be fair. Men are just as guilty of poor communication about their needs. What a man says and what he means can be two totally different things as well. Ladies, I think you'll appreciate these examples.

> **He says:** [In response to the woman asking him if he needs help with a difficult, challenging chore] No, I got it.
>
> **He means:** Of course I need help, but I'm a man and I can't ask for help. I'll do it myself. I'll be angry and irritable for the next several hours, but I will get a tough job done with no help.
>
> **He says:** Honey, I loaded the dishwasher [or washed your car, did a load of laundry, fixed that doorknob for you, or any chore he's done around the home].
>
> **He means:** I'd love for you to thank me for doing this chore. I can't ask for a compliment right to your face because that would make me feel weak and embarrassed, but I need your praise. If I don't get it, I'll sulk and I won't tell you why.
>
> **He says:** [In response to the woman asking him how he feels] Fine.
>
> **He means:** I am fine, but I don't want to talk about why I feel fine [or I'm not fine, but I don't want to talk about why I don't feel fine].
>
> **He says:** What are you doing tonight?

He means: I want to have sex.

He says: Is your period over?

He means: I want to have sex.

He says: I want to talk with you in the bedroom.

He means: I want to have sex.

He says: [Nothing at all about sex all day. At the end of the day when you're coming out of the bathroom, he smiles and pats your pillow.]

He means: This is your lucky night, sweetie. You get to have sex with me.

Sound familiar, ladies? I thought so. How can you meet your man's needs when he doesn't make them clear? The answer is you can't.

My examples of how men and women fail to communicate needs are designed to be humorous. But there's nothing funny about a couple whose needs go unmet month after month after month. When needs aren't met in a romantic, committed relationship, a destructive chain reaction is created:

- ❧ Needs go unmet.

- ❧ Frustration, hurt, anger, and rejection result.

- ❧ Partners drift further and further apart.

- ❧ More and more needs go unmet.

- ❧ The relationship dies.

How Are We Doing?

- To which of my examples of poor communication of needs do you relate the most?

- Can you admit that you don't make your needs clear to your partner?

- How do you feel when your needs aren't met? How do you react? What do you do and say?

- Tell your partner which of your core needs are not being met. Then tell your partner which of your secondary needs aren't being met.

- How do you communicate your needs, both core and secondary, to your partner?

HERE'S WHAT WE CAN DO

For the first ten years of our marriage Sandy and I were not effective at communicating our needs. We still loved each other, but our love was taking some serious hits every day.

It finally dawned on us that the best way to stop the deadly chain reaction of unmet needs resulting from our communication failure was to arrest the problem right at the beginning of the chain. How? By identifying each partner's needs, both core and secondary, throughout each day.

Our daily need-meeting system has made a huge difference in our relationship. We are convinced it will do the same for you and your partner.

Step 1: Ask in the morning.

In the morning, before you go your separate ways, ask your partner what her or his needs are for that day. I recommend that the man asks first. Then the woman asks the man. Checking in with each other like this is a beautiful way to express your love. When you ask, your partner knows you truly care, and you both will find it easier to share your needs.

And—I'm stating the obvious here—this way both sets of needs are identified as the day begins. No confusion. No miscommunication. Record your partner's needs for the day, and commit to meeting them that day. If you can't meet a need, say so immediately.

This initial sharing of needs is best done in person, but other methods can be effective as well. If you don't see each other early in the morning, no problem. That's why you have your phone. Make a call or send a text.

You might say:

- "Please pick up Susie at school today."

- "Run by the grocery store and get a half gallon of nonfat milk and a dozen large eggs—open the carton and check them."

- "I'd like to make love tonight."

- "Would you call the mechanic about my oil change?"

- "I need you to clean the bathrooms tonight."

Step 2: Communicate any changes.

As the day unfolds, stay in touch via phone, and communicate any changes to your needs. You may change your list of needs at any time. You may remove one of your needs from your partner's list, or you may add a new need to the list. If you realize you can't meet one of your partner's needs, let him/her know right away and give the reason.

For example:

> ❧ "I'd prefer to get Susie myself after all."

> ❧ "Please also get granola bars and baked beans—an eight-ounce can."

> ❧ "Skip the bathrooms—two loads of laundry would be better."

Step 3: Report your stress.

Give your partner updates on your stress level throughout the day, especially if it is rising significantly. Your stress level may impact your ability to meet your partner's needs, may change your own needs, and will certainly impact your evening together. Knowing when your partner is angry, upset, or irritable helps you to be better prepared to provide understanding and comfort when you reunite after the workday.

Here are some examples of stress updates:

> ❧ "My boss just chewed me out, and I'm angry and scared."

> ❧ "I'll be late getting home and can't get the groceries."

> ❧ "Now I *really* need to make love tonight!"

> ❧ "Let me unwind alone for twenty minutes when I get home; then we'll talk about what happened."

Step 4: Ask in the evening.

When you first lay eyes on each other after the day, do four things right in a row: (1) give each other two or more kisses, (2) say, "I love you," (3) give each other a compliment, and (4) ask what your partner's needs are for that evening. If you've kept in contact during the day, you should know the needs and any changes. But if you haven't had contact, you want to find out if there have been any changes.

For example:

🐾 "Johnny needs help with his math homework."

🐾 "I have to run to the drugstore—please start dinner."

🐾 "After the kids are in bed, let's talk—first about your stressful day and then about what's happening with my parents and their health."

Is this need-meeting system simple? Yes, very simple. Is it effective? Yes, very effective. It doesn't take much time and allows you to clearly identify your partner's needs over the course of a day. And when needs are identified, they can be met.

What Will Block Us?

- What part of this approach will be the biggest challenge for you? Why?

- Talk about your daily schedules and responsibilities and how you can work around them to follow this system.

- Does it seem as though I'm asking too much of you? If yes, why?

- Would becoming angry with your partner keep you from asking about his or her needs and working this system?

- How difficult will it be to share your stress level with your partner? What may happen if you don't share your stress?

LET'S PRACTICE

I want you to follow this daily need-meeting system for three consecutive days. Expect it to be difficult. Expect there to be problems. Don't get discouraged. You are establishing a new pattern, and you have to work out the kinks.

For three consecutive days:

- Ask each other about your needs in the morning.

- Communicate any changes to your needs throughout the day.

- Alert each other to your stress level during the day.

- Follow up with each other in the evening.

How Did We Do?

- Did anything go wrong over the three days? What was the most difficult part of this approach to carry out?

- What was harder—identifying your partner's needs or meeting them? Were there any surprises or revelations?

- If your partner's needs changed during the day, how did you deal with the changes?

- What went right with this approach? What needs got met? How did it feel to meet your partner's needs and receive praise? How did it feel to get your needs met?

- Are you ready to commit to following this strategy each day?

- If you take a day or a few days off from following the need-meeting system, are you willing to get back on track with it?

ESSENTIAL AREA 7

WE NEED TO TALK ABOUT OUR SINS AND WEAKNESSES+

CHAPTER 12

ALONE YOU FAIL, TOGETHER YOU SUCCEED

*T*HE FIRST WORDS I say at my emotional health seminars are designed to send a jolt through my audience. I want those listening to feel nervous. I want them to sweat. I want them to fight the urge to cry out for their mamas.

Believe me, that's exactly what happens. When I take the platform, I say:

> I'm going to begin with a brief demonstration. I'm a highly trained professional psychologist. I'm trained to identify and treat emotional problems. In fact, I am so well trained, I can actually tell if a person has an emotional problem just by looking at him or her. I will now point out those of you who have emotional problems.

At this point I leave the platform and walk right into the audience. I stroll slowly down the center aisle, scanning the crowd carefully. There's a lot of nervous laughter, and the intensity in the room can be cut with a knife. Suddenly every single person has a serious case of ants in the pants. There's more fidgeting going on than you'd find in a kindergarten class. Bottoms are squirming, eyes are darting, and lips are being licked.

I can see from their panicked expressions what they are thinking:

- ҉ Is this guy crazy?

- ҉ He's not serious, is he?

- ҉ Does he have some kind of special powers?

- ҉ Maybe if I look normal, he'll pass me over.

- ҉ Mama! Help me, Mama!

- ҉ I know I shouldn't have worn this purple lip-stick; he'll think I'm nuts for sure.

- ҉ I think *he's* the one with the emotional problem!

The next words out of my mouth put everyone at ease. I say:

> Actually, it's very easy. *You all do.* Every person in this room, including me, has an emotional problem.

The fear and nail-biting anxiety evaporate. All the tension washes out of the room with a beautiful *whoosh*. With three simple words—*"You all do"*—I have connected with my audience. I have communicated what they've desperately needed to hear: *We're all in this together.*

NOBODY'S NORMAL

The only person who ever lived on earth who did not have an emotional problem is Jesus Christ. He suffered terrible pain and experienced sadness and anxiety, but He never developed an emotional problem. He was—and is—the healthiest person in the history of the world.

But you're not Jesus. You have an emotional problem.

Here's my definition of *emotional problem*:

> An area of weakness and potential serious sin that if not controlled, will destroy you and all your close relationships.

Check out this list of emotional problems. I bet you'll find yourself on it:

- Food: overeating, bulimia, anorexia

- Sex: pornography, physical or emotional adultery, lack of interest in sex, inordinate or unfair demanding of sex

- Gambling

- Alcohol: misuse or addiction

- Drugs: prescription or illegal

- Anger: verbal or physical abuse

- Work: being lazy or working too much

- Kids: spending too little or too much time with them

- Exercise: working out obsessively or neglecting to keep fit

- Hobbies that take up way too much time

- Spiritual apathy

- Overinvolvement at church

- Reticence: clamming up and refusing to communicate

- Overattachment to pets: putting them before your partner and other close relationships

- Control issues: needing to control or manipulate people or circumstances

- Jealousy

- Obsessive use of a smartphone, tablet, or computer

- Compulsive checking of social media

- Excessive playing of video games

- Sports: spending too much time playing or watching them

- Excessive reading that starves your close relationships

- Excessive watching of television

- Use of cigarettes or chewing tobacco

- Compulsive desire to shop or spend money

- Compulsive need to save money

- Excessive pursuit of power or fame

- Untreated depression, anxiety, obsessive-compulsive disorder, or bipolar disorder

- Poor self-esteem

- Neglect or abuse in the past: physical, sexual, or verbal

ॐ Codependency

ॐ Extreme selfishness

ॐ Inability to commit in romantic relationships

Your weakness is on this list, isn't it? Or maybe it isn't since this isn't an exhaustive list by any means. But be honest and admit that you have an emotional problem. You have one. I have one. (Actually, I have more than one!) We all have one. And if it's not controlled, it can lead to serious sin.

WORK IS MY EMOTIONAL PROBLEM

Let me get personal because I'm not going to ask you to do something that I'm not willing to do. My main emotional problem is work. "Hi. My name is Dave, and I'm a workaholic."

I love to do therapy in my office. I love giving telephone and e-mail advice. I love presenting my seminars. I love writing books. I love doing media interviews to promote my various ministries, and I love offering help to people.

I love my work too much. It has done damage to my relationships with Sandy, my kids, my family, my friends, and God. My workaholism was particularly out of control when the kids were small and I was building my practice.

With Sandy's help I learned to control my work and keep my schedule balanced. It wasn't easy. It still isn't easy. Sandy and I work as a team to help me avoid sinning in my work life. A great bonus is that working together (since my secretary of twenty-five years retired) has produced a wonderful intimacy.

SIN LURKS HERE

Your emotional problem may be a sin: an addiction, outbursts of anger, selfishness, and so on. Or your emotional problem may not be a sin—yet. If you don't heal and get into solid recovery, your emotional problem will certainly lead to sinful behavior. If I work hard but prioritize my wife and kids, I do not sin. But if I overwork and neglect my wife and kids, I sin.

If you were abused in the past, you did not sin. Your abuser sinned. But if you don't heal from the abuse and forgive your abuser, then your unresolved pain from the abuse will lead to sinful behavior: a need to control others, mistrust of your spouse, chronic jealousy, depression that keeps you from intimacy, and so on. Deal with the emotional problems now so they don't lead to sin in the future.

How Are We Doing?

- Identify the emotional problem of each person in your family (grandparents, parents, stepparents, siblings).

- What did each family member do to control his or her emotional problem? What damage did you see these emotional problems cause?

- Think of friends and coworkers, and discuss with your partner the damage their emotional problems have caused in their lives.

> • Tell your partner what your emotional
> problem is—the area in which you are
> tempted to sin. For now just mention it. We'll
> go into more detail about what to do next in
> the next few pages.

HERE'S WHAT WE CAN DO

I'm going to recommend you do something that will scare you.

It's something that 99 percent of couples do not do. It's something the Christian community doesn't talk about. It's also something that will protect you from serious relationship sin and give you a deep level of intimacy.

What I want you to cultivate—and what I'm convinced God wants you to have—is a *wide-open, vulnerable* relationship. A relationship characterized by complete and total honesty about your individual areas of weakness.

That's right. I'm urging you to reveal to each other the sinful behaviors that Satan is most likely to tempt you to do. It's time to talk about your sins, whether they are still in the potential stage or in full-on destructive mode.

No more secrets. No more covering up. No more denial. No more lies.

In many cases your sin is obvious, and your partner knows exactly what you're doing. Whether your sin is out in the open or hidden, sit down with your partner and disclose everything you know about your damaging behavior. When it started. Why you think it started. The unresolved past pain that may be the source of your sin. What specific acts you have done or thought of doing up to now in your area of sin. Give the details.

Identify the current triggers that set you on the path to committing your sin. Talk about the ways Satan goes about tempting you to sin. Discuss the rationalizations you use to excuse and justify your sin. Go over why you continue to sin or think of sinning in this area. What does it do for you? What are the payoffs? What needs are you trying to meet in your life by committing your sin?

Talk about your guilt and shame. Admit that you're wrong and you're sincerely sorry for your sin and the pain it has caused your partner and your family, as well as the pain and grief and dishonor it has brought to God. Describe the damage your sin has done to you, your relationship with God, and your relationship with your partner.

Allow—even *invite*—your partner to vent his or her feelings about your sin and its impact on your relationship. Allow your partner to ask as many questions as necessary to form a complete picture of your sinful behavior. Healing and the beginning of trust will come through the many private conversations you have about your sin.

Ask for your partner's ongoing help in dealing with your sinful behavior pattern.

Commit to telling your partner anytime you are seriously tempted to sin in your area of weakness. Commit to telling your partner whenever you are beginning the rationalization process on your way to committing this sin. You know when you're in real trouble and when you are close to sinning.

Agree with your partner that at the point of heavy-duty temptation or rationalization, you will call him or her before you act on your desire to sin. If necessary you will wake your partner out of a sound sleep. You will share the struggle you are having with your temptation.

In response your partner will agree to speak the truth in a loving way. Your partner will support you and give you added strength to gain the victory over your temptation. Agree with your partner that the two of you will pray together when tempted and ask for God's help that He has promised in 1 Corinthians 10:13 and 2 Peter 2:9. It will be the two of you and God against Satan (Eccles. 4:9–12; Matt. 18:19–20).

I'm not suggesting you reveal to your partner every temptation or sinful thought that comes into your mind. That would drive both of you crazy. But when you are really struggling with recurrent, potentially harmful thoughts and you are in real danger of acting out those thoughts, you need to tell your partner what's happening.

Keep in mind, not just one of you is going to be totally honest about your areas of sin. *Both* of you are because both you have an area of potential serious sin. The literally almost continuous battle between us and sin exists in us all (Gal. 5:17–18.) That's why you support each other. That's why you pray for each other. With a loving spirit you hold each other accountable.

You may need another accountability partner, such as a friend of the same sex. You may need a Christian therapist. You may need a Christ-centered addiction recovery group, such as Celebrate Recovery. But your most important teammate and accountability coach in your ongoing battle with your sinful behavior pattern is always going to be your partner.

Now let's pause a moment to check in. Are you freaking out yet? Are you feeling massive anxiety? Are you thinking,

What are you, nuts? I can't tell my partner the details of my sinful behavior and give an update every time I'm in serious temptation mode. That's way too personal! It's also risky. The truth will hurt my partner terribly and may even lead to a separation or even divorce. Our relationship will never be the same. I'll just handle it myself.

If you're thinking this way, join the club. Every couple to whom I've recommended this wide-open, vulnerable relationship plan has voiced these same protests.

Here are my answers.

First, if you don't enlist your partner in battling your temptation to sin, you'll continue to sin. You cannot handle serious sin on your own. Your sin will end up handling you. Your sin will severely damage your relationship to the point of ending the relationship. The divorce rate among Christian couples—those who say they know Jesus personally—is about 50 percent. This rate is the same as among non-Christian couples. Isn't it time for a different approach?

Second, even if your partner never discovers your sin—which is unlikely—the cover-up and secrets will separate you from each other. Your sins will always be a black hole between you. Secrets separate. Truth connects.

Third, when your sins are on the table and you're working as a sin-defeating team, you will create an amazing intimacy. Talking about your feelings of temptation to sin and about sins you are committing or have committed is incredibly personal and connects couples on a deep level. If you can talk about your temptations and sins, you can talk about anything. And you will! Your openness about your sinful patterns will spread to every other area of your lives. Your communication will reach levels you never dreamed possible.

I know it takes guts—real guts—to do what I'm asking you to do in this chapter. I hope and pray you do it because the benefits to both of you personally and to your relationship are enormous.

If you don't feel ready to share this deeply and honestly, do three things: (1) Pray about it. (2) Seriously evaluate your feelings toward your partner: Do you love him or her enough to be this honest? (3) Move through the rest of the chapters of this book and then come back to this one, ready to get honest.

What Will Block Us?

- What is your reaction to the wide-open, vulnerable relationship I am proposing?

- What are you afraid will happen if you're totally honest about your area of weakness and sin?

- Have you ever revealed the truth about a sinful habit to someone? If so, how did it go? Did the person handle your truth well, or did you get burned? Explain.

- A deep level of honesty requires a deep level of commitment. Are you committed to each other enough to share honestly?

LET'S PRACTICE

I hope you have already revealed your area of weakness and sin to your partner. Now in a series of conversations this week I want the two of you to go deeper:

- ◈ Describe in detail your sinful, damaging behavior—how and when it started, why you think it started, and what you've done up until now to sin in this area.

- ◈ Identify the triggers that cause you to sin, the ways Satan tempts you, your rationalizations, and the payoffs for you of your behavior.

- ◈ If your area of weakness has not yet caused damage, talk about the damage it could cause.

- ◈ If your sin has already caused damage, describe that damage and ask your partner to describe the damage he or she has felt.

- ◈ Invite your partner to vent any and all feelings about your sin and its impact on the relationship. Allow your partner to ask all the questions necessary about your sin. If a lot of damage has been done, be willing to spend weeks, even months, having these venting/questioning conversations.

- ◈ Agree to team up with your partner in battling your sinful behavior pattern. Commit to telling your partner when you are seriously tempted to sin in your area of weakness.

- ◈ Give your partner permission to call you on your area of weakness when he or she sees the danger signs. Also allow your partner to ask you at any time how you're dealing with your weakness.

To be clear, I want both of you to follow these steps. Once one partner has completed these steps, the other partner will follow them.

How Did We Do?

- What was the most difficult, painful step in this process?

- How do you feel now after telling the truth?

- Are you both willing to continue being honest about your areas of weakness and sin? Do you believe it's worth the pain and the risk?

- If you need extra help to get into recovery from your sinful pattern of behavior, are you willing—this week—to make an appointment with a Christian therapist? Are you also willing to get a same-sex accountability partner and attend a Christ-centered recovery group?

ESSENTIAL AREA 8

WE NEED TO TALK ABOUT
OUR FINANCES

CHAPTER 13

MONEY MELTDOWN OR
FINANCIAL FREEDOM?

*E*VERY SATURDAY MORNING I pay the bills. When the children were at home, everyone knew to stay away when I sat down at the dining room table in front of my huge stack of bills. Let's just say I get a little crabby.

I hate paying the bills. Hate it, hate it, hate it. I'd rather take a beating. I hate everything about the miserable, painful process.

I hate watching my bank account balance shrink as I subtract each bill's amount—all that hard-earned money getting sucked out, one bill at a time.

I hate having to fill in the amount of the bill on the receipt. The bill states, "Please fill in the amount you're paying." Well, what other amount would I put in there? Often I'll write by the amount, "Duh!"

I hate having to write the incredibly long account number on the check. (Yes, I write checks. I hate the Internet and computers too.) Could they make those account numbers any longer? Besides, they already know my account number; it's on the receipt I'm sending to them!

Although I hate all my bills, I especially loathe my life insurance bill. It comes to me every two and a half months. And it's not cheap. I hate paying it because I get nothing in return. I have to die before there is a payoff. As I pay this nasty bill, I actually *feel* like dying so I can get some money out of the insurance company. Plus when I'm dead, I won't have to pay this bill—or any other bill!

Some years ago our oldest child, Emily, was sitting at the dining room table as I paid the bills. Brave girl! I said to her, "Honey, you need to ask two questions of the young men you date. First, do you know Jesus? Second, will you pay the bills for me?" Emily thought I was kidding. I was not kidding.

Paying the regular bills is bad enough. But as you know, it doesn't stop there. Something is always breaking. The air conditioner breaks. The refrigerator breaks. The toilet breaks. The car breaks. The arm of one of your kids breaks.

It's always something. And every something costs you money. Just when you think you have a chance to get ahead and keep some extra money in the bank, something happens and you kiss that extra money good-bye.

MONEY STRESS GOES UP
IN A RELATIONSHIP

When you're single, your money stress is high. But when you're living with a spouse, your money stress is doubled. Maybe even tripled. Why? Because now you have to work with someone else to make all kinds of money decisions: How much to spend, how much to save. What to buy, what not to buy. How much debt is acceptable to both of you. The list of money decisions goes on and on.

All these decisions are brutally tough because of your differences. Each partner has a unique, firmly entrenched view of money. That's OK when you're single. It becomes not OK when you couple up. Now your two views of money will clash. Repeatedly.

The Spender and the Saver

In 95 percent of the couples I've seen in therapy, one partner is the Spender and the other is the Saver. This is not a pretty combination. It is, financially speaking, a nightmare scenario that causes couples ongoing conflict.

Here's a breakdown of these two money types:

SPENDER	SAVER
I want it, I need it, I buy it.	I don't want it, I don't need it, and so I don't buy it.
I decide to buy quickly.	I take weeks to research a purchase.
I am emotionally attached to the things I buy.	I am emotionally attached to my money.
I want to live for now, to spend money while we can enjoy it.	I want to plan for the future. I don't intend to spend until I'm eighty.
I want to spend on entertainment: eating out, movies, vacations.	I want to stay home and save money.
We don't need a lot in savings. What if one of us dies?	We need a big amount in savings because what if we *don't* die young?
I can't be bothered balancing our accounts; I'll take the bank's word for it.	I balance the accounts to the penny every month; you can't trust banks!
What's a budget? Is that a rental car company?	We need a budget so we can track all of our expenditures.

Do you see any potential problems in this Spender/Saver scenario? I know you do because like most of us you're living it. The Spender and the Saver do battle over just about every aspect of their finances.

Money can't make you happy. In fact, "the love of money is the root of all evil" (1 Tim. 6:10, MEV). But it can certainly make you unhappy and break you up.

The Remodeler and the Curator

In our marriage Sandy is the Spender and I am the Saver. Of course, I'm so unbelievably cheap that anyone would look like a Spender compared to me.

One of our ongoing financial conflicts is what to do in our home. Sandy is always thinking of ways to remodel and make our home more attractive and functional and exciting. She is the *Remodeler*.

Sandy wants new appliances. Hardwood floors. New kitchen cabinets. New granite countertops. New tile in the bathrooms. She even wants to take down the wall between the kitchen and the dining room.

I see our home as a museum, and I am the *Curator*. I want it to stay exactly as it is. I mean, why spend a fortune when our home is just fine the way it is right now? I want to preserve our artifacts—Sandy would say *antiquities*—for generations to come.

This is just one area in which our Spender/Saver difference bites us. We've had to learn to communicate regularly about money and make compromises to protect our relationship.

The two of you will have to do the same thing, and I'm going to help you do it.

How Are We Doing?

- In your relationship who is the Spender and who is the Saver?

- Spender, what feeling does spending give you? What do you spend money on?

- Saver, what feeling does saving give you? What are you saving money for?

- In the area of finances what do you argue about the most?

- Who is better at handling the bills?

- How much debt do you have? Who do you owe?

- What kind of savings plan do you have? Are you putting money into retirement accounts?

- Do you tithe on a regular basis? If not, why? If you do, how often and how much do you tithe? Where does your tithe go?

HERE'S WHAT WE CAN DO

I'm no financial wizard, but Sandy and I have learned some things in the money arena of our relationship. I'm going to share four simple principles that have helped us deal with money in a fairly harmonious way. Sure, we still have conflicts over money (now she wants a new home!), but these principles make conflicts manageable.

Additionally, I'll share that I am a Dave Ramsey fan. In my opinion he is the top Christian authority on financial issues. If you are just starting out and want to establish a firm financial foundation, if you are struggling with money, or if you just want to improve as a couple in this vital area, get Dave's materials. Attend his Financial Peace University program. His practical wisdom will make a huge difference in your financial world.

Here are the four principles we've adopted and found to be successful.

Principle 1: One partner pays the bills and handles investments.

Almost always one partner is significantly better at handling the money. This person may not like the job; in fact—like me—the money manager may hate the job. But this partner is the better choice to deal directly with all money matters.

This partner is typically the Saver. This partner is organized, self-disciplined, task-oriented, and able to create structure. These are the traits that make a good money manager. You don't want a dreamy, spontaneous, free-spirit type in charge of the finances.

The money manager is responsible for all the financial jobs in the relationship: tracking and paying the bills, saving money, making investments, funding retirement accounts, paying down debt, and tithing.

Even though this partner takes care of the money, teamwork is crucial. I do all the jobs above, but I discuss with Sandy every aspect of every financial job. First, we talk about each category on a regular basis. Second, I follow through and implement *our* decision.

I tell her what bills I'm paying and the amounts. If we're having a tight month, I let her know, and together we decide how to cut expenses. If I have to delay paying a bill or take money from savings to pay a bill, we talk about it before I do it.

We thoroughly discuss the amount we intend to save each month, the specific investments we make through our financial advisor, the amount we want to put into our retirement accounts each month, the plan we follow to pay off debt, the amount we tithe, and the organizations and ministries we support with our tithes and offerings.

Principle 2: Get out of debt ASAP.

The crushing weight of debt has killed, and is killing, millions of marriages. Debt not only ruins your credit score; it also ruins your relationship. Debt severely limits your financial options, causes tremendous stress, and creates loss of trust, respect, and security between you—and sooner or later loss of love.

Sandy and I have avoided debt as much as possible by not buying things we don't need and can't afford. We do use a credit card, but we pay off the entire balance every month. We work hard to use the credit card only to buy things we actually need and would buy anyway with cash.

For big-ticket items, such as our office building, cars, new air conditioner unit (see, Sandy did get something new for the home!), and college tuition for the kids, we have gone into debt. These were critically important needs that we couldn't pay for up front and could not be delayed. But we are striving to pay off these debts as soon as possible.

We have implemented a plan of debt reduction. Each month I pay more than necessary on each debt. We're encouraged to see the debt amounts going down. Plus the sooner we pay them off, the sooner we stop paying interest.

Principle 3: Make monthly contributions to retirement accounts.

When our four kids were small—pre–elementary school age—Steve Murray, our trusted financial advisor, sat us down and said, "Dave and Sandy, you need to start planning and preparing for your retirement. You're young now, but you won't be young forever. Pay yourselves every month. Settle on a figure to save, and send me a check for that amount every month. Over time your retirement accounts will grow."

Boy, was that great advice. Despite all the expenses we faced providing for four kids and also contributing to a college fund, we committed to Steve's plan to make monthly contributions to our retirement accounts. We still do it. It hasn't been easy, but we feel much more secure about the future.

Principle 4: Tithe.

Although I'm discussing tithing last, it really ought to be first. Sandy and I believe that every cent of our money is God's and not ours (Job 41:11; Ps. 24:1; Hag. 2:8). We *ourselves* are not our own; we were bought with a price—the death of Christ (1 Cor. 6:19–20.) We believe that our tithes and offerings every month ought to be paid first, *before* all the other expenses (Neh. 10:35–37). We believe it is biblical to give 10 percent of all we earn (Gen. 14:20; Heb. 7:1–10), and to give extra money as God prospers us (1 Cor. 16:2).

Since the New Testament teaches the primary place of the local church in God's plan to take the gospel to the world and because of the church's role in the individual lives of His children, we believe it is right to give most of our tithes and offerings to the local church.

As the Bible teaches will happen (2 Cor. 9:6–15), God has blessed us richly for our giving through tithes and extra offerings to the local church and Christian ministries. He has blessed us financially, that's true. But more importantly He has blessed us spiritually with a closer love relationship with Him.

What Will Block Us?

- Which of you handles the bills? Is it working well, or does the other partner need to take over?

- Do you struggle to have honest conversations about money? When you do talk about money, what is the tone of the conversation?

- How do you feel about your debt? How badly do you want to pay off your debt?

- What stops you from making regular contributions to your retirement accounts? How much do you think you will need for a secure retirement? How much or little can you put into retirement now?

- If you don't tithe, why not? If you do tithe, what percentage of your income do you tithe?

LET'S PRACTICE

All right, it's nitty-gritty time. It's never fun to talk about money, but you need to do it. You can't fix something—or improve it—if you don't talk about it.

This week I want the two of you to have three thirty-minute conversations about money. One conversation isn't enough because money is an extremely sensitive, complicated issue. Your approach to money includes not only your present views about money, but everything you learned in your early years.

Identify which one of you is the better person to be the money manager. Talk about your finances and the main concerns each of you has in this area. Agree to talk regularly about all aspects of your finances: how you are spending your money, paying the bills, going about debt reduction, making investments, funding retirement, and tithing.

Talk about your debt and how each of you feels about it. Talk about what you saw in your childhood home regarding money.

Nail down exactly how you plan to reduce and eliminate your debt.

Discuss your retirement. How much do you have in your retirement accounts? How often and how much do you contribute to these accounts? Agree on a specific figure— no matter how small at first—you should contribute to your accounts every month.

Talk about tithing. Are you both comfortable with the amount you are presently giving to God? How often and how much do you tithe? How much do you believe you ought to be giving? How much do you *want* to give to God? Remember, "God loves a cheerful giver" (2 Cor. 9:7). Jesus Himself said, "It is more blessed to give than to receive" (Acts 20:35).

How Did We Do?

- What was the most difficult, painful topic in your financial discussions?

- What is your main weakness when it comes to money? Ask your partner to tell you what he or she thinks is your main weakness. Alone, ask the Lord what He thinks.

- Which financial area needs the most work?

- Commit to talking about money on a regular basis: as needed for financial decisions and at least once a month to evaluate where you are in your handling of money.

- If tithing and giving extra money to God is an issue, agree to talk to your pastor or the pastor of a good friend or family member and hear what the Bible teaches.

- If you are struggling with money in your relationship: First, join the club. Second, start using Dave Ramsey's materials together and develop a solid, biblical plan for your management of money.

ESSENTIAL AREA 9

WE NEED TO TALK ABOUT OUR PARENTING

CHAPTER 14

THESE KIDS ARE DRIVING US CRAZY!

I TAUGHT FOUR TEENAGERS how to drive a car. Do you know the kind of courage that requires? Running into a burning building, rescuing a swimmer from a riptide, or staring down a group of Hell's Angels bikers—none of these exploits demands the raw, gutsy courage necessary for getting into a car with a teenager at the wheel.

Though I taught all four of my kids to drive, I'm going to focus on William. He's our only son and the baby of the family.

Being a boy and being William, he had supreme confidence in his ability to drive a car. This confidence had absolutely no basis in reality since he'd never driven a car in his life!

After a few laps around our neighborhood I let William drive in actual city traffic. I will never forget those first five or six trips. I've tried—with extensive therapy and heavy medication—to forget them, without success.

I tried to project a calm demeanor, but terror lurked within. I realized I was sitting in the "death seat," and my life was in the hands of a fifteen-year-old boy who had no idea what he was doing.

I developed TMJ from constantly clenching my jaw. I got carpal tunnel syndrome from repeatedly grabbing my seat and the dashboard. And of course I got whiplash from the abrupt stops and starts.

William didn't take instruction well. In response to my warnings and teaching comments, he'd say things like, "How dare you criticize my driving? I'm an excellent driver. I'm a better driver than you."

My response was, "Really? I've been driving for thirty-five years. You've been driving"—I looked at my watch for emphasis—"about twenty minutes. How can I not know more about driving than you?"

William had a bad habit of driving too close to the right side of the road. I'd be sitting there watching mailboxes whiz by just an inch from our car. When I pointed out how close we were to them, William retorted, "Would you rather I hit the mailboxes or the oncoming traffic?"

I responded, "Well, if those are my only two choices, I choose the mailboxes. But can we miss both the mailboxes *and* the oncoming traffic? Is that possible?"

All I can say is that it was a good thing I wore adult diapers when in the car with William.

I'm happy to report that William is now an excellent driver. And I've recovered from my nervous breakdown. I'm out of the mental ward and back to a fairly normal life.

My point with this story is that teaching a teenager to drive is a metaphor for the parenting process:

> ₰ It is very important.

> ₰ You face a lot of resistance and many obstacles.

> ₰ It is terrifying.

> ₰ It is exhausting.

ॐ It is largely out of your control.

ॐ It is costly. (When I called my auto insurance company to put William on our policy, the woman I talked to actually laughed out loud—a real gut laugh.)

ॐ You don't know how it's going to turn out.

WHERE THE RUBBER MEETS THE ROAD

In my personal and professional experience I have witnessed the many facets of parenting. The challenges of parenting are many. I've seen parents struggle to raise healthy kids while building careers, taking care of the home, dealing with their own parents and other family members, serving in church, paying the bills, and maintaining an intimate marriage.

I've seen strong-willed kids who defy their parents and do not respond to the typical, standard parenting advice. I've seen brothers and sisters who hate each other and engage in out-of-control sibling rivalry. I've seen blended families that do not blend.

I've seen parents battle each other because they have very different parenting and discipline styles. I've seen parents try to control all the social media outlets that are available to their kids. And I've seen parents who must deal with teenagers who are addicted to Internet pornography.

I've seen parents cope with schools that openly teach liberal, sinful values and lifestyles. I've seen parents struggle to instill godly values in their kids in a world with no godly values.

I've also seen the joys of parenting. I've seen the faces of parents with their newborn child. I've seen kids develop their unique personalities. I've seen the pride of moms and dads at their children's sporting events, dance and music recitals, plays, martial arts matches, and band and choir performances.

I've seen parents laugh their heads off at the funny things their kids say and do. I've seen parents joyfully witness all the firsts in their child's life: first step, first day without diapers, first day of school, first day of camp, first day of driving alone (an event that brings joy and terror!), first date, first day of college, first time believing Jesus Christ died for their sins and rose again.

With all its challenges, sorrows, and joys, parenting is quite an adventure. I want to help you two be the very best parents you can be.

A CRASH COURSE IN PARENTING

In this chapter I'm going to teach some key principles of effective parenting. These principles have helped Sandy and me and many parents I've worked with in my therapy office and at my seminars. You will get practical help no matter what kind of parent you are: biological, adoptive, foster, or in a blended family. Even if you don't have kids yet, the material in this chapter will be excellent preparation for parenthood.

Of course, in these few pages I can cover only a fraction of parenting wisdom. For my contribution to the field of parenting, get my comprehensive parenting manual, *Winning the Parenting War*.

How Are We Doing?

- What is going well in your parenting? What strategies are working?

- What is not going well in your parenting? What are your greatest challenges or struggles as a parent?

- What mistakes have you made as a parent? Ask each other to name some of the mistakes you feel the other has made, keeping in mind that you both will make mistakes.

- Talk with each other about each of the children. What are their strengths and weaknesses?

- If you could improve one thing in the life and behavior of each child, what would it be?

- If you don't have kids yet, what are your main fears about raising kids?

HERE'S WHAT WE CAN DO

I'm going to share with you the three most important actions Sandy and I took as our four children grew up. These intentional behaviors made a huge difference in our lives and the lives of our children.

Action 1: Make your relationship number one.

Make sure your husband-wife relationship is the most important relationship on the face of the earth. If you don't, two very bad things will happen: (1) your relationship will fail, and (2) your children will suffer because your happiness is the single most vital plank of security in their lives.

The Bible, our instruction manual for living a successful, happy life, is clear that marriage is the most important human relationship. Genesis 2:24 states the fundamental truth that in marriage husband and wife become "one flesh," a complete unity. It is a relationship established by God Himself. This union is the foundation of the family.

Marriage is God's plan for men and women in serious romantic relationships. If you truly love each other and can create genuine intimacy, God wants you to get married. If you have children, God wants you to raise them under the protection and security and love of the marriage.

Ephesians 5:25 says marriage is the very picture of Christ's relationship with the church—that is, those who have believed in Him. Wow! Because Christ gave His life for us, our love in the marriage relationship is to be completely sacrificial and unconditional.

Well, case closed. Marriage is the most important human relationship. Nowhere in the Bible does even a relationship with a child reach this level of significance and sacredness.

So how do you make your relationship number one? You actually already know how to do this. All the preceding chapters in this book have taught you the skills necessary to build a deeply intimate bond:

- Make time to communicate and learn how to communicate

- Create spiritual intimacy

- Handle your conflicts successfully

&♥ Heal from your past unresolved pain

&♥ Practice positive and romantic behaviors

&♥ Meet real needs

&♥ Team up against your areas of weakness

&♥ Put in place a solid financial plan

Action 2: Communicate love to your children every day.
I define *love* this way:

> The feeling that you belong, that you are uncondition-
> ally accepted by at least one person in your life.

Without love you have nothing. Without love you are nothing. To be loved is the greatest human need.

Your children have a desperate need to be loved by you. They need to *feel* your love. Love is an action; *doing* things communicates love. Here are three daily actions through which you can communicate your love to your kids.

Say "I love you."

These are beautiful words. Powerful words. Healing words. Every day that your children are growing up, say these words to each one of them. Use the child's name: "I love you, Bobby." "I love you, Susie."

I hear from clients every week these sad words: "My dad and my mom never said to me, 'I love you,' as I grew up." As a result these persons have poor self-esteem and feel unlovable. Often they will do almost anything—sometimes even something self-destructive—to "earn" the love they should have received in their home. *Don't let this happen to your children.* Say "I love you" every day to every child in your family. When they hit middle school, they won't say

191

it back to you for a few years. That's OK. Keep on saying it every day.

Give physical affection.

What's the largest organ in the human body? Skin! Why are we covered with skin? Because it is meant to be touched! God could have covered us with sandpaper or barnacles, but He didn't do that.

Touch feels warm. It feels caring. It feels like love. At least once a day touch each child in an affectionate way, with a hug, a kiss, a squeeze of the shoulder, a brush of the hair, or a pat on the back. Even a low-key, brief touch communicates love.

The older kids get, the harder it is to touch them. They develop a personal space bubble and act as though they don't need Mom and Dad to touch them. The truth is that as they move into middle school and high school, they need touch from you more than ever. For many kids, maybe most, the teen years are the period of lowest self-esteem—despite their actions to the contrary. Sneak up on them if you have to, and give a brief touch. And keep doing it every day.

Share your spirituality.

Bonding spiritually with your children is a wonderful way to express your love for them. It also is a powerful way to teach them about God and how all-important He is in your life and in their lives.

Every day Sandy and I took these three spiritual actions with our four kids.

First, in the morning before they left for school, we'd pray briefly with each child that God would bless and guide her or him during the day.

Second, at dinner one of us would pray and thank God

for each child and for the meal. During the meal, one of us would share something in the spiritual area. We would thank God for an answer to prayer, share a verse from our devotional time that morning, or talk about how God guided us that day.

Third, at the end of the day, just before bedtime, we each spent a few minutes praying with each child. We'd thank God for that child, thank Him for the day, and pray for whatever our child wanted to pray about. Of course, when they got older, they didn't necessarily want this brief end-of-day prayer time, and they didn't share many prayer requests. To be sure, we prayed for them anyway.

If you are a stepparent…

Now just a word about blended families. First, many excellent books and materials are available by those with experience in this area, and I recommend you seek these out. But I'll go ahead and say that as a stepparent you will likely find it harder—quite a bit harder—to express love to your stepchildren in these ways. But you have to do it, and you have to keep doing it.

Never stop trying to build a relationship with your step-children. Keep loving on them and loving on them and loving on them, no matter what their response is. They can be rejecting, critical, and mean. They can be cold and withdrawn. They can ignore you. They might say:

꙰ "I hate you."

꙰ "I want you to go away."

꙰ "I want you to die."

꙰ "I want to break up this marriage."

&❧ "You're not my mom!"

&❧ "You're not my dad!"

Whatever. Keep loving on them in the ways I've recommended.

And don't ever forget: Your relationship with your spouse is a joy to you. But to the children it may represent the opposite: sadness, one parent gone, or worse, a broken home. This is a challenge you have accepted and must meet and win.

By showing love to your stepchildren, you are showing love for your partner, who is their biological parent. Your partner will notice your efforts and love you for them.

Showing your love for your stepchildren will pay off down the road. As adults they will often warm up and appreciate how you never gave up on loving them.

One of the most awful things I hear in my therapy office is when a stepparent says to me, "I'm giving up on that kid. I'm done trying to build a relationship." Don't ever say that. If you have said it, take it back, apologize, and start expressing love again.

Action 3: Develop an effective discipline strategy.

The third action I urge you to take is in the area of discipline. Working together as a couple, create the House Rules. Develop and write down reasonable behavior standards and reasonable rewards and consequences.

If the children choose to follow your standards, they will be rewarded. If they choose to disobey your standards, they will receive consequences. Now you can't put down on paper every possible behavior standard, but you can cover the main areas: chores, homework, respect, character traits, treatment of siblings, expectations around friends, limits on social media and television, and moral and spiritual values.

When a child—whether your biological child or a stepchild—chooses to disobey, put the child on hold, and the two of you parents talk about it. The two of you should always talk privately and reach a mutual decision. When you come back from your conversation, you must be in total agreement: "This is *our* decision."

When it comes to blended families, discussion of a child's misbehavior should always be done in private with the biological parent, never in front of the other children. And keep in mind two essential principles regarding the blended family: First, the biological parent should always have the final say on discipline; the stepparent has full input but does not have authority to make the decision. Second, the biological parent delivers the consequence. As a stepparent don't make the classic mistake of disciplining a stepchild on your own. Otherwise you will be met with terrific resistance and resentment. The biological parent disciplines the biological child—period.

What do you do as a stepparent when the stepchild acts out and the biological parent—your partner—isn't around? First, try to reach your partner by phone or text. If that effort fails, discipline in the name of the biological parent: "I believe your mother/father would want this action to be taken."

What Will Block Us?

- Be honest: Are you putting your children above your partner? Ask your partner if he or she feels you are. If you are, why do you think you are?

- What will be hard about making your partner number one in your life? What do you fear will happen if you make this change?

- Which of the nine essential areas covered thus far in this book is the most challenging for you? Why is this area so difficult for you?

- What gets in the way of saying "I love you"? Of giving physical affection? Of talking about spiritual matters with your children? Which of these will be the hardest for you? Why?

- If you don't apply consequences when your children disobey, why don't you? Why are you too soft on them?

- If you are too hard on your children, why do think you are that way?

- What will keep you from working with your partner as a team in the difficult area of discipline?

- If you don't have kids yet, what areas of parenting do you think will present the biggest challenge for you?

LET'S PRACTICE

This week, I want the two of you to have a talk about how to make sure your relationship is being given more importance than your kids. If you're focused on your kids, admit it. Discuss how you've done so far in the essential areas covered in this book. Has your work in these essential areas made your relationship a greater priority and led to a deeper level of intimacy?

Do the three love actions—saying "I love you," giving physical affection, and sharing your spirituality—with each of your children every day this next week. If you are a blended family, do them with each of your partner's children too. If you're not with each child every day, you can still call or text "I love you" and share a prayer or something spiritual with them. That's what smartphones are for!

Have another talk this week about the area of discipline—how you're doing, what's working, and what's not working. Develop a plan of reasonable rewards and consequences for each child. You may not get all these plans carried out, but you will have started the process.

When a child chooses to disobey this week (which will happen), practice going through my suggested plan of discipline.

How Did We Do?

- What will you do to make the one you love number one? What is one action you can take this week to make your partner your top priority?

- Which of the three love actions was the most difficult for you? Why?

- What impact did the three daily love actions have on each of your children? How did you feel doing these actions?

- If you're a stepparent, were you able to make progress in building a better relationship with your stepchildren? Are you willing to commit to continuing to work on these relationships, no matter what?

- What was the toughest part of coming up with a discipline plan for your children? How well did you work together on rewards and consequences?

- How did you do at following the suggested steps after a child has disobeyed? What was hard about the process?

- If you have serious issues in your family, are you willing to see a Christian professional therapist to work on them?

- If you don't have kids yet, discuss the challenges you believe you will face in making your marriage your top priority once you do have a child.

ESSENTIAL AREA 10

WE NEED TO TALK ABOUT OUR PHYSICAL INTIMACY

CHAPTER 15

NAKED, NOT ASHAMED, AND HAPPY IN BED

I'M SITTING HERE wondering, *Why are so many married couples unhappy with their physical relationship? We have two persons who are physically attracted to each other, love each other, and want to make love. I mean, what could possibly go wrong with this natural, beautiful experience?*

You know me well enough by now to realize I'm not being serious. I know exactly why so many couples are struggling in the bedroom. It's because of the many incredible differences between a man and a woman.

The two of you are:

- Different sexually
- Different physically
- Different hormonally
- Different intellectually
- Different in brain construction and chemistry
- Different in emotional expression
- Different in personality
- Different in family background
- Different in the desired frequency of sex

    ❧ Different in how long it takes to get sexually
       aroused

    ❧ Different in what it takes to get sexually
       aroused

    ❧ Different in how orgasm occurs

All these differences make sex challenging enough. But it doesn't stop there. Add your jobs, day-to-day stress, the speed of life, family responsibilities, home and automobile maintenance, bill paying, and the million little things you both have to do to keep your lives and relationship running at least sort of smoothly, and the ability to connect sexually grows even more challenging.

And then you go and have a child. What were you thinking? Now your sex life is in real trouble. The child is always around and has a ton of needs that never end!

You know what? I'm surprised *any* couple is having great sex. I'm surprised any couple is having sex at all!

You have physical attraction obviously, or you wouldn't be together. You also love each other, and that's good. But physical attraction and love are not enough to create a consistently passionate and meaningful sex life. Not by a long shot.

Just as has been the case with the previous nine essential areas we've covered, to be successful in your physical relationship, you need to (1) talk honestly and openly—in detail—about sex and (2) follow a game plan for improvement. If you don't do these two things, nothing will change in the bedroom. Actually your sex life *will* change. It will get worse and worse until you're not having sex at all.

LET'S TALK ABOUT SEX

Let me state the obvious: it can be, and usually is, difficult and super awkward to talk about your sex life. Sex is an extremely private and sensitive topic. It is a time when you are at your most vulnerable. Here are some common concerns I have heard from couples in my private practice and my responses:

> **Client:** I'm afraid I will really hurt my spouse if I tell the truth about our sex life.
>
> **Me:** You will really hurt your spouse if you don't tell the truth about your sex life. Things will only get better if you talk honestly about what is happening in the bedroom.
>
> **Client:** I'm afraid I will make my spouse angry if we talk about sex.
>
> **Me:** No, I don't think so. If you speak in a loving, kind way with a clear emphasis on wanting to improve your lovemaking, anger is rarely the response. If your spouse does get angry, you have bigger problems than your sex life.
>
> **Client:** Shouldn't sex just be natural? Why do we have to talk about it?
>
> **Me:** You're kidding, right? No area of marriage comes naturally, unless it's making mistakes. You have to work at sex to get the most out of it, and that means talking about it.
>
> **Client:** Our sex isn't great, but at least it's working. I'd hate to make it worse by talking about it.

Me: I hope you don't settle for mediocre sex. It doesn't take long for mediocre sex to become lousy sex. You cannot make it worse by talking about it. You will make it worse by not talking about it.

Client: I'm afraid that if we talk about sex, my spouse will ask me to do sexual things I don't want to do.

Me: That could happen, but you have every right to explain why you don't want to do certain sexual actions. Talking about sex will settle these matters and put your mind at ease because you won't have to worry about being asked to do them. And with honest dialogue you two can get past unhealthy blocks and—with mutual agreement—try new things in your sex life.

One important message before we go further. If you are a couple and not married, the information in this chapter will be great preparation for your future sex life. In God's plan sexual intercourse is only to take place when you are married. So you two will be applying and practicing only the section on emotional and spiritual connection. Read the other sections for informational purposes, but I don't want you to practice these sexual actions until after you are married.

Now, let's take a closer look at your physical relationship.

How Are We Doing?

- Rate your physical love life on a scale of one to ten, with one being nonexistent and ten being fantastic.

- What is good about your physical relationship?

- What is not good? What is not working for you in the bedroom?

- If you're struggling to achieve sexual pleasure and satisfaction, what do you think is impeding you? What has changed to make sex less enjoyable, less exciting, less fulfilling?

- Ask your partner what you can do to better meet his or her physical intimacy needs. Ask your partner to give you detailed scenarios so you can know precisely what to do differently (assuming it is mutually acceptable).

HERE'S WHAT WE CAN DO

You probably won't be surprised to hear that I have four practical steps you can take to get your sex life back on track and keep it on track. These steps aren't theory. I know they work. They've worked for Sandy and me and for many other couples who have come to me with sexual problems.

Step 1: Establish an emotional and spiritual connection.

Great sex requires great preparation. Great preparation means connecting emotionally and spiritually prior to intercourse. News alert: sexual pleasure does not begin in the bedroom! We actually make love in the kitchen, the living room, and the car, and while we're walking, talking, and eating. Sex is not merely a physical act. It is an emotional and spiritual act, as well as a physical one.

All a man needs for arousal is to see his wife's naked body. His arousal is immediate and caused by the visual. If only the woman could get aroused immediately by seeing her husband naked. That would be a perfect sexual world for us men.

Of course we don't live in a perfect world. The woman becomes sexually aroused through emotional and spiritual connection to her man. Deep conversation and spiritual bonding through prayer and spiritual sharing play a big role in producing in her a passionate desire for her man.

Bummer! all you guys are thinking. But actually it's not a bummer. The man needs these emotional and spiritual connections just as much as the woman. When you bond as a couple in these two areas, the walls between you come down and you both are ready for great sex.

I've already taught you how to connect on these emotional and spiritual levels in chapters 1–5. Follow the guidelines I offer in these chapters in your three Couple Talk Times each week, and the frequency and passion of your sex will go way up. It won't be just the regular, run-of-the-mill, mediocre sex; it will be intense, stimulating, fun sex.

Step 2: Schedule your intercourse.

Wouldn't it be fantastic if you could have sex spontaneously whenever the mood strikes you? You walk into the kitchen on a weekday morning and kiss your woman passionately. She purrs, "You want me, don't you? I want you too—bad. I can't wait until tonight. No, really. I can't wait, and I won't wait. Let's make sweet love right now."

All right, it's time to leave Fantasy World. Join Sandy and

me in Reality Land, where life is busy and a thousand and one daily obstacles get in the way of making love.

Spontaneous sex is a slim-to-none proposition when you don't have kids. Have even one child, and it becomes an absolute impossibility. Children are wonderful, but they cramp your sexual style big time.

It's true: scheduling sex will lead to better sex. Why? First, because scheduling it will ensure you have it. You can't have better sex if you're not *having* sex, you know? Plus you'll have it much more often.

Second, scheduling sex helps you both to get ready for your physical time together. You'll have time to connect emotionally and spiritually in one or two Couple Talk Times. You'll save your energy so you're not exhausted by the time you reach the bedroom. And you'll enjoy the anticipation and get yourself in the mood.

A quick word about kids and not allowing them to ruin your sex life: if your children are small, get them to bed early on the evenings you have planned to make love. (In fact, get them to bed at a decent hour every night, so you have time to build your relationship.)

If they keep coming out of their rooms, lock them in. I'm not kidding. We had a deal with our small kids: stay in bed, and your door will stay open; leave your bed, and your door will be closed and locked. If a child's door was locked, we left a night-light on, and later in the evening we'd open the door.

If your children are older, they will already be in their rooms in the evening—because they hate you. (I'm kidding, of course.) Simply tell them to stay in their rooms for the next hour because Mom and Dad will be having a special time together. Upon hearing this message, your teenagers will go throw up in the bathroom and run back to their rooms. They'll lock their doors, play loud music, hide under their covers, and mumble to themselves over and over, "They're just talking in there. They're just talking in there. They're just talking…"

One more thing: put a heavy door with a dead bolt on your bedroom. You want to make absolutely certain that no one—children, other family members, intruders, or houseguests—can get into your love nest.

Step 3: Focus on foreplay.

There are times when you're forced to have a "quickie." You've missed a few opportunities for sex, and so when you get a brief window ("Johnny's at the neighbor's house, and Susie's piano lesson will last another twenty minutes"), you seize it. But these times should be the exception and not the rule. This kind of speedy sex is more difficult for the wife to pull off, but it means a lot to the husband. Men, make sure you show your appreciation for these times.

Great sex requires time in foreplay. Without foreplay the sex act itself isn't particularly endearing or meaningful. Do you know what I mean? Extended foreplay is fun, exciting, and a unique, God-designed, super way of showing love, and it gets you both prepared for intercourse.

Caressing, touching, kissing, massaging, and fondling are all important. Foreplay is truly making love and leads to increasing levels of arousal for both the man and the woman.

Foreplay should last at least twenty-five to thirty minutes, or until both partners are sufficiently aroused and ready for orgasm. Keep in mind, men, that the average woman takes close to a half hour to reach full sexual arousal and to reach readiness for orgasm. In fact, most women do not achieve orgasm in the act of intercourse; thus, for the woman, foreplay is of great importance, and her husband should be eminently aware of this fact.

Extended foreplay has many benefits. The woman becomes aroused and lubricated. The man becomes even more aroused. The woman may have an orgasm. She will feel that the sexual experience is not just about the man, but about both of them. This time before intercourse is extremely enjoyable and is a wonderful way of expressing your love. And it leads to a more intense and pleasurable orgasm for both husband and wife.

The "afterglow," the time following orgasms, is particularly important to the woman. Continuing to kiss and share loving words at that point means a great deal to her. Among other things it assures her that her husband is not just interested in the physical act but truly loves her and wants her for herself.

Step 4: Work together on your sexual problems.

You will struggle sexually at times. All couples do. Agree right up front that it's always *our* problem—it is never *your* problem or *my* problem. In my experience as a clinical psychologist, it's just as common for the man to struggle in this sensitive area as it is for the woman. You face the problem together, and you work through it together.

If you are unable to resolve a sexual issue, go together to a Christian licensed therapist who has expertise in the area of sexuality. Sexual problems can often be symptoms of individual or relationship issues. A number of personal issues could be the source, such as abuse as a child, unresolved issues with an ex-spouse, stress, performance anxiety, depression, or poor self-esteem.

In the relational realm, conflict and tension between partners can easily—and quickly—damage and kill the sexual relationship. Scripture's instruction is "Be angry, and yet do not sin; do not let the sun go down on your anger, and do not give the devil an opportunity" (Eph. 4:26–27, NASB). Add to that these profound words from God: "Be kind to one another, tender-hearted, forgiving each other, just as God in Christ also has forgiven you" (Eph. 4:32, NASB).

Sometimes sexual problems have a physical origin. To rule out this case, see a gynecologist or urologist to get a thorough checkup.

Do not—*do not*—let a sexual problem go and try to move on without coming to a mutually satisfying solution with your partner. What you are missing will not correct itself.

As with all ten essential areas, honest communication is the key to success and intimacy. Have regular conversations—at least once a month—about your physical relationship. What's going well? What would each of you like to change?

When you hit obstacles and difficulties in bed—and you will—talk about them and take steps together to fix them. Any reluctance to talk about sex indicates the need for immediate conversation and a search for answers.

What Will Block Us?

- How are you doing with your emotional and spiritual connections each week? Are you doing your three Couple Talk Times each week? Are you having deeper conversations? If not, why?

- Are you bonding spiritually by praying together and sharing your individual spiritual lives? If not, why?

- How many times on average are you having intercourse each week? Tell your partner how often you'd like to have intercourse. What would make you not want to schedule these intimate times?

- Discuss your foreplay. How long does it tend to be? Are you both sufficiently aroused before intercourse? If foreplay is shorter than twenty-five minutes, why is that?

- What keeps you from having honest talks about your sex life? When was the last time you had a good talk about your sex life? What do you think will happen if you talk about it on a regular basis?

- What will stop you from seeking professional help for sexual problems?

LET'S PRACTICE

Schedule three Couple Talk Times this week. Work to connect emotionally and spiritually. If you hit obstacles to these connections, talk about them and about what you can do to improve.

Schedule at least one lovemaking appointment this week. Two would be even better if the desire is mutual. Since one of you will likely forget, put the appointment(s) on your fancy, state-of-the-art electronic device. When it beeps, it's time for sex!

Make sure your foreplay lasts as long as the woman wants it to be—at least twenty-five minutes. You can use an egg timer or program your smartphone to go off at twenty-five minutes. (Kidding.) Make foreplay last until you *both* are sexually aroused and say you're ready for intercourse.

Have at least one very open, detailed talk about your sex life. It could take place during a Couple Talk Time. Discuss how each of you feels about your lovemaking, how much each of you is enjoying it, and what each of you likes the best or would like to add or change. If you're having problems, gently talk through them and agree to take action to fix them. Be sure to discuss any sources of discontent outside of the sexual relationship that may be hurting the physical relationship.

How Did We Do?

- How did your Couple Talk Times go? Are you getting deeper emotionally and spiritually? Evaluate each Talk Time you had this week, and discuss what went right and what went wrong.

- How did the scheduling of sex go? Was it easy or difficult to do? Did you follow through and make love at the appointed times? If not, why?

- Did you engage in foreplay for at least twenty-five minutes? Was the woman fully satisfied with the amount of time it was given? If an extended time of foreplay was hard to pull off, why? Discuss your foreplay and how it can be improved.

- What was the result of your detailed talk about your sex life? When having this talk, how did you both feel?

- If you're still struggling sexually, are you both willing to seek professional help? Will you commit to working together until you resolve the issues?

WHERE TO GO
FROM HERE

CHAPTER 16

ARE WE BREAKING UP OR GETTING MARRIED?

HERE COMES A time in every romantic relationship when the two persons have to decide whether to break up or get married. We've reached that time in this book. If you are in a significant romantic relationship but not married— if you're dating seriously, engaged, or perhaps even living together—by the end of this chapter, you'll be ready to make the decision to end the relationship or get married.

One of the following five scenarios should fit your situation.

SCENARIO 1: "WE ARE READY TO GET MARRIED"

This is the good-news scenario. You have worked your way through the book and feel confident that marriage is the next step. Maybe you have just confirmed what you already knew and the book has only deepened your love. Or maybe the book revealed some areas of weakness yet brought both of you to an increased level of closeness and the realization that you want to get married. In either case, you are now better prepared to move toward marriage. Congratulations!

SCENARIO 2: "WE CAN'T GET CLOSE"

In this scenario you both have gone through all ten essential areas outlined in this book and done all the hard work

I've asked you to do (well, not *all* the hard work; sex is meant to be experienced within the context of marriage). But the result is that you've still not reached a deeper level of intimacy. Despite your best efforts your relationship has stayed pretty much the same.

You've come to realize there are limitations on the closeness you experience in certain areas of your relationship. You do love each other, and you may want to get married, but I have to tell you: marriage is not the right decision.

Amicably and with great care and sensitivity, you need to end the relationship. It will be hard—very hard—but you will never be able to reach deeper levels of intimacy in your relationship. In my professional experience the honest conversations and intentional actions in these ten areas reveal the quality of your relationship. Either you will connect on a deeper level or you won't. More time together won't make a difference. Love is not enough. You can be very good friends, but you'll never be passionately and deeply in love.

SCENARIO 3: "MY PARTNER REFUSES TO WORK THROUGH THE BOOK"

If you are in this situation, your decision is easy—very painful, but easy. This book has been a catalyst to expose your partner as a fraud.

He—and I'll use the masculine pronoun here, though it could just as easily be the woman—is not into you and does not love you. His refusal to work through this book with you is beyond insulting. It means you are not worth anything to him—not even as little as the work in this book would require to help make a marriage and a lifetime of happiness possible. You are a convenience, not a forever partner, to him.

The truth is intimacy requires commitment. He doesn't have it. Intimacy requires honest talks about everything in your relationship. He won't have these talks. Intimacy requires a lot of ongoing, hard work. He refuses to do that work. If he won't even go through this book with you, based on my experience, he certainly won't do any other work on the relationship.

Given the present circumstances, he will never be into you and will never love you. He is not committed to you and never will be. It will hurt to say good-bye, but it will hurt a whole lot more to stay with someone like this.

Get out. And get out now.

SCENARIO 4: "MY PARTNER IS BLOCKED"

In this case you have been working steadily through the ten essential areas together—that's no small task; you deserve medals!—but your partner has gotten blocked in one or more of the areas. She—and I'll use the feminine pronoun here for balance—is unable or unwilling to do all of the work and answer all of the questions outlined in that area.

This scenario is not uncommon, given the challenge this process no doubt has presented to both of you. But it is unacceptable for her not to work through all of the essential areas with you. Every area we've covered is important and can't be missed. Believe me when I tell you that the one area your partner will not address is the same area that will kill your relationship.

At this point ask your partner to go back and work through the challenging area with you. It's possible that the work you've now accomplished in the other areas will give her the confidence she needs to do the work in the sensitive area.

But if she still says she's unable to deal with that area, it's clear she has a deeper issue that must be faced in therapy. Ask her to go with you to a Christian licensed therapist. With this specialized help she can—with your full support and involvement—heal from the unresolved pain connected to this area of her life. Without an involved, expert person outside of your relationship, nothing will change.

Here's the tough part. If she refuses to see a therapist with you, walk away from the relationship. Her unresolved issues will prevent the two of you from achieving real intimacy. Plus her refusal to deal directly with this one area will spread to other situations and problems in your relationship. How many other issues will she refuse to work through with you?

If you walk away and she decides she can't live without you and will see a therapist, go through the therapy process together. But if she won't see a therapist, stay away from her and move on.

SCENARIO 5: "WE STILL CAN'T COMMIT TO MARRIAGE"

In this last scenario the two of you have worked through all ten essential areas together and have done well. You have developed a deeper level of intimacy. However, that deeper level of emotional and spiritual intimacy has not translated into a deeper level of commitment.

One of you still is not ready to commit to marriage. Or it could be that neither of you feels ready for marriage.

But it is still true that once you've worked hard to create an intimate relationship, the next logical step is marriage. In the world of relationships, marriage is the pinnacle. Marriage is the best plan for two persons who are in love. I say so based on my thirty-three years of marriage to Sandy and my work in private practice with couples for thirty years.

But much more importantly, God says so:

> Therefore a man will leave his father and his mother and be joined to his wife, and they will become one flesh.
> —GENESIS 2:24, MEV

God created marriage; it is His idea. He instituted marriage—a monogamous, heterosexual union. Jesus quoted the above verse and declared that this relationship is to be permanent (Mark 10:7, 9). *One flesh* describes the ultimate, the best, the deepest kind of intimacy possible between a man and a woman. You can experience one-flesh intimacy only in marriage.

If you genuinely love each other and have achieved intimacy at this point in the book but still aren't sure about getting married, something's wrong. To help you get past your reservations, let's take a look at the classic reasons people give for not getting married—and my responses.

"I Don't Want to Get Married Because _____"

> **You:** My parents' marriage was awful. They were so terribly unhappy. I lived with that for eighteen years, and it has really turned me off marriage. I don't want to be stuck in a marriage like theirs.

> **Me:** I hear you, and I get it. Who wants a marriage like that? But yours doesn't have to be like that. Your parents chose to be miserable and do nothing about it. You and your partner can create intimacy and have proven you can deal successfully

with the challenges and problems in a relationship. You haven't completely healed from what your parents did to you, and that is preventing you from building a relationship/marriage that is the opposite of your parents' marriage.

You: My ex burned me badly, and I never want to go through that kind of pain and rejection again. A breakup is one thing; a divorce would be a lot worse.

Me: The end of a relationship, whether you were married or not, causes a lot of pain. And it might happen again. But you and your partner have done the work in this book, and your relationship is solid. You have examined your relationship and acquired essential tools to keep building it strong and beautiful for as long as you live. Yes, marriage is a risk. But it is a good risk. You shouldn't stay unmarried because of the risk. Life is full of risks. And you haven't completely healed from what your ex did to you.

You: I love my partner, but I don't know if he/she is the one.

Me: If you've been close for at least a year and you don't know if they're the one, then they're not the one. And you don't love them that much. Do yourselves a favor, and break up.

You: I'm a very independent person.

Me: You can be independent and married. In successful, happy marriages the two persons can handle life on their own quite well but because of love chose to enter a relationship in which the partners are equals. You continue to have your life, but you choose to put your partner's needs and well-being above your own. If you can't do that for your partner, break up.

You: I've seen too many family members, friends, and coworkers get divorced. It looks to me like marriage isn't working out for many couples.

Me: There's nothing wrong with the institution of marriage. The problem is the persons in the marriages. With hard work and God's help your marriage can be a happy, healthy, successful one.

You: It makes sense to try out marriage by living together first. Most of our friends are doing this.

Me: It seems to make sense, but it doesn't make biblical sense. God's plan is marriage, and His Word clearly instructs men and women to keep sex for marriage. And because of this truth, living together violates God's rules (1 Thess. 4:3; Heb. 13:4). And it doesn't, in fact, make practical sense. Living together doesn't, in fact, lead to a stronger and more intimate relationship. How many of your friends are any closer to getting married by living together? Are their relationships becoming more and more intimate and committed? Or are they staying pretty much the same or deteriorating?

You: Marriage just isn't working anymore. Very few couples seem to be really happy for a lifetime. I just don't think any marriage can last.

Me: You've bought our culture's lies that marriage is outdated and that marital love never lasts. There are couples whose marriages remain intimate and vibrant for a lifetime. The media rarely mentions these happy couples. Find a few of them and ask them what has worked for them.

You: I'm not ready to commit for life.

Me: With the right person and a relationship based on honest communication and the skills developed in the ten essential areas covered in this book, you will expectantly leap at a life sentence. Since you've worked through these ten essential areas and still aren't ready for a lifetime commitment, get out of the relationship. You're either all in or all out. You're all out, so break up.

You: I may not marry my partner, but I'm committed.

Me: No, you're not committed. You have zero commitment. You can leave anytime you want to leave. Commitment is marriage—saying, "I promise I will love you for as long as I live."

These are the popular reasons I hear from clients who don't feel ready to move their relationship to marriage. You may have other reasons not to get married. Whatever the case, I want the two of you to have a series of honest talks about marriage. Share and discuss in detail your reasons for not wanting to get married. Lay it all on the table—no holding back to try to protect yourself or your partner.

If these truthful conversations do not lead to a firm desire and commitment to marry, go together to a reputable Christian therapist. Work with the therapist on the deeper reasons for your lack of commitment. Therapy can identify the obstacles to the commitment of marriage and get you past them.

If therapy, both as a couple and as individuals, doesn't lead to a breakthrough, break up. You're not that into each other, and you need to admit it and move on.

If your partner won't see a therapist, break up. By refusing to work with a therapist and explore commitment issues, your partner is sending a clear message: "I don't want to be committed to you."

MARRIAGE IS THE GOAL

I guess you've noticed by now that I am powerfully pro-marriage. Why? Because God is powerfully and irrevocably pro-marriage. Marriage is God's plan A. Actually, that's not true. Marriage is God's *only* plan for two persons who love each other. He offers no other options.

You and I have a choice. We can trust Him completely, or we can choose not to and follow our own plan. But what is the track record of couples following their own plans? Abysmal.

God is not the God of dating forever. He is not the God of endless engagement. He is not the God of living together. He is the God of marriage.

Marriage offers the maximum amount of commitment, love, passion, joy, and security possible in an opposite-sex relationship. Marriage offers you the best in a romantic relationship from the one true God. Marriage is a sacred relationship in God's eyes. He will always bless your efforts to improve your marriage and grow your love.

I didn't write this book so you could have a better dating relationship or a better engagement experience or a better living together relationship. I wrote it so you could grow deeply in love and make the choice to get married.

I know it's a tough message, but here it is again in a nutshell: work through the ten essential areas covered in this book, and then break up or get married.

CHAPTER 17

WHEN YOUR SPOUSE WON'T COMPLETE THIS PROGRAM WITH YOU

I BELIEVE WORKING THROUGH the content of this book can dramatically improve a relationship. You'd expect me to believe this, of course, because I wrote it! I've taken hundreds of couples, married and unmarried, through this process of focusing on the ten essential areas we've covered, and I've seen it work over and over again.

It will work for you and your partner too—*if* you both are willing to follow all the steps.

This chapter is for those of you who are married but have a spouse who doesn't want to participate in the program I've outlined here. My suggested approach for you is quite different than what I proposed in the last chapter to those who are not married. As you read in the previous chapter, I have no problem recommending that unmarried couples break up if one partner refuses to take part in this program. If you're not married, your relationship is not sacred to God and there is no biblical mandate to stay together.

If you are married, your relationship is sacred, and the Bible teaches that you are to do everything possible to stay married. Not once in my thirty years as a psychologist have I recommended divorce. And I never will. (Just to be clear, I don't encourage spouses to remain in abusive situations, but even in such cases, once the abused partner is in a place of safety, the decision to divorce should be made very prayerfully.) Marriage is God's ordained institution and a beautiful, wonderful gift to us. God hates the harming or the ending of this union (Mal. 2:16). Jesus said, "What therefore God has joined together, let no man separate" (Matt. 19:6, NASB). Divorce is entirely, solely humankind's idea. God alone can say if a spouse may be released from a marriage. If God decides to release you from your marriage, He will make this clear to you.

After reading the previous chapters, do you agree that the steps outlined in this book can generate breakthroughs in communication and real intimacy in your marriage? If your answer is yes, it is important that you and your spouse go through the ten essential areas together. As you already know, the book is designed for use by couples. While you may glean some benefits reading the book on your own, the significant benefits come only by working through the book together.

My theory, based on experience, is that a decent, loving spouse will agree to complete the book's steps with you. A reluctant spouse, however, may require some motivation to get past resistance to my program.

IF YOUR SPOUSE HAS SAID NO TO THE BOOK

Usually a spouse's no comes in one of these forms:

1. He or she doesn't want to read the book or complete any of the steps.

2. He or she says yes but gets blocked in one or
more of the ten areas—and won't see a therapist to get unblocked.

3. He or she says yes but does it in a lazy, half-
hearted, superficial, "I'm doing it because I
have to" way.

When you get one of these no answers, you immediately
need to take a series of progressive action steps to motivate your spouse to go all in and join you in completing
the reading and assignments. If you don't take action, your
spouse will never complete the book with you, and you'll
lose an excellent opportunity to deepen your relationship.
If you take these action steps, there's a good chance your
spouse will join you in working through the book.

Step 1: Get God and one other person on your team.

As you begin your campaign to motivate your spouse,
you need encouragement and prayer. Lean on God and pray
that He will touch your spouse's heart and cause him or her
to want to do the book with you.

Also, ask someone—a close friend or an older, wiser
mentor of the same sex—for prayer support. Tell this person
what you're trying to accomplish in your marriage and ask
him or her to pray with you for a successful outcome.

Step 2: Set up the first meeting.

I'm going to assume the spouse in this scenario is the
husband. Wife, go to your husband, ask him to sit down in
a private place in your home and in a deadly serious tone
say these words:

[His name], I have something very important to talk
to you about. It's about our marriage. I'm not ready
to talk about it now. I want the kids out of the house
when we talk. Let's meet in three days, on [day of
the week].

After you schedule the meeting with him, get up and go
about your business. If he asks what this is all about, tell
him you'll explain everything at the meeting.

Spend the next three days being a bit quieter and more
reserved than normal. You want him to wonder—even
worry—about what you are going to say. You want him
to realize that the topic of this meeting is very important
to you.

Since he recently has said no to working through the
book, he may guess the meeting is about that topic, but give
no indication of what you're going to talk about until the
time for the meeting comes.

Step 3: Conduct the first meeting.

On the appointed day of the meeting, when you are both
settled in, here is what you say to him:

Honey, I'm going to speak for a few minutes. Please
don't say anything; just listen to me.

Our marriage is not where I want it to be. I believe
we can be much more intimate and have a deeper
love. I want to be close to you. We can have a great
marriage. But it will take work.

I think Dr. Clarke's book can really help us as a
couple. Your resistance to reading the book and completing the steps has made me feel frustrated and
hurt. I feel as though you don't care about me and my
needs as your wife.

I'm asking you to do something for me, for you, and for our marriage. What I want you to do in the next seven days is read the introduction and first three chapters of Dr. Clarke's book. You can read more if you want to, but at least read these four chapters. They will give you a good idea of Dr. Clarke's style and his overall plan.

In one week let's meet again, and I want to hear your reaction to the chapters. We'll talk about any questions and reservations you might have about the book and Dr. Clarke's steps.

OK, I'm done. I don't want to hear your feelings and thoughts now. Take this next week and, in addition to reading the four chapters, think and pray about working through the entire book with me.

When you're done with your statement, get up and move on with your regular activities. You won't discuss the book until the next meeting. You'll remain quiet and serious for the next seven days.

If he comes to you before the next meeting and in a genuine and heartfelt way expresses a desire to work through the book, go ahead and start the book with him. He's clearly a good guy, he loves you, and he gets how important this process is to you. He's now on board, and you're good to go.

Step 4: Have the second meeting.

In the second meeting ask him to give you his honest response to the four chapters he has read. You want to hear his position on going through the book with you.

If he starts the meeting by agreeing—with a good attitude—to complete the book with you, then your meeting will be a short and happy one. You'll say thanks and set a time to talk about chapter 1.

If he still offers resistance, that's OK. It's discouraging, but it's acceptable. You asked for his input, and you will listen to all of it.

Here are some classic responses of resistant spouses and how you can respond to them:

> **Resistant Spouse:** You know I don't read. I hate to read. Isn't there a video or DVD we can watch?
>
> **You:** I know you can read. I've seen you read the back of cereal boxes. And the sports page in the newspaper that has both letters and numbers. You read texts on the phone, don't you? This book will get us a lot deeper than any video. I'm asking you to read the book for me and for us. Am I worth it to you?
>
> **Resistant Spouse:** This process could take a while. It'll take me time to read. And there's a lot of homework.
>
> **You:** Anything of value takes time to achieve. We have plenty of time. There's no time limit. We can complete the chapters at our own pace. It's probably better to go slowly anyway so we can learn the skills as we do each step.
>
> **Resistant Spouse:** We don't need this book. Our marriage is fine.
>
> **You:** Would I be asking you to do this if I thought our marriage was fine? And besides, do you want to settle for less than the best we could be together? You wouldn't settle for a "fine" career, would you? I know you want to do as well as possible at work.

Well, our marriage is much more important than work. Let's go for a great, passionate marriage!

Resistant Spouse: Talking about all these areas will be awkward and really difficult for me.

You: Yes, it will be awkward and really difficult for me too. But if we avoid these areas, our relationship is going to get into trouble. It won't be easy, but our marriage is worth it.

Resistant Spouse: What if we don't agree in some of the areas?

You: We will disagree, but that's normal and OK. We will be expressing our real feelings, our individual truth. We can't be right or wrong. We'll find ways to compromise. Plus Dr. Clarke included a chapter on how to resolve conflicts.

Resistant Spouse: What if we can't communicate on a deeper level?

You: Just by following Dr. Clarke's process and talking openly and honestly about these ten areas, we'll learn to communicate on a deeper level. With God's help I know we can improve our communication and closeness and happiness.

Resistant Spouse: I don't talk deeply. That's not who I am. You knew that when you married me. I can't change.

You: Really? You're going to go with the old "I was like this when you married me" excuse? I'm not buying it. If you love me, you'll change. You're smart, and you can learn how to open up and talk more deeply and personally. I have my own hang-ups in communication. We'll learn together how to get deeper.

Resistant Spouse: Some of the areas in the book are just too private. I can't go there. It's too painful. I think talking about these areas will just make matters worse.

You: Honey, I'm your wife, and I want to help you face these sensitive areas. Some of them are the very obstacles to our happiness. If we don't talk through them, they will continue to hurt you and limit our relationship. Some of these areas will be painful for me too. Let's do it together.

(You can ask him to read these resistance responses directly from these pages—along with the answers I've written for you—especially if you find it hard to verbalize my comebacks.)

If, at the end of this second meeting, he still seems resistant to working through the book, you will have to get out the big guns. Tell him:

I want you to spend the next seven days thinking about and processing all we said today. I want you to pray that God will reveal to you what is stopping you. I believe our marriage should be a priority for us both, so pray and ask God what has messed up your priorities and His priorities in your life and what He wants you to do about this. Talk to your dad or a close male friend about the book and what I'm asking you to do. Talk to our pastor. Talk to a Christian therapist. Think about what is more important to you: me or protecting yourself. In a week I want your final answer—yes or no—about working through the book with me.

I've found that most spouses will respond positively—and pretty quickly—in one of the first two meetings. They are good people. They do love their spouses. So they will do the book.

If, however, after those seven days your spouse still says no to the book, you may have a problem. His saying no to the book is acceptable if he offers a reasonable alternative. If he is willing to see a Christian therapist or follow another book's approach, that's OK.

But if he says no and gives no other options for working on your marriage, it's clear the challenges in your marriage are more significant than communication. If your spouse knows your needs aren't being met and refuses to do anything about it, he is putting himself and what he wants above you and the marriage. And that is sin. Ephesians 5:25 says a husband is to love his wife as Christ loves the church. This means showing his wife unconditional love and making her needs his top priority after his relationship with God. (Although this verse focuses on husbands, it is just as wrong for a wife to refuse to address areas in the marriage that are causing her husband pain.)

In my counseling practice I take men and women in this situation through specific steps to get to the root issues plaguing their marriage. A spouse's refusal to help meet his or her partner's needs is a sign that a marriage is in serious trouble. But this book is not written for this scenario. If this is your sad reality, get my book *Married but Lonely* for a detailed description of the tough-love steps you need to take.

CHAPTER 18

IT'S ALL UP FROM HERE

*Y*OU FINISHED! WELL done. Working through these ten essential areas wasn't easy, was it? I'm proud of you, and I'm confident God is proud of you.

By speaking openly and honestly with each other in these ten areas, you have:

- ❧ Broken down barriers and resistance to closeness

- ❧ Connected on a deeper level

- ❧ Come to know your spouse much better

- ❧ Gained a new set of relationship skills

- ❧ Learned how to achieve real spiritual, emotional, and physical intimacy

- ❧ Proven that you can talk about any topic, anytime, anywhere

So many couples cannot and do not talk about certain topics. So they do not come to compromises in those areas. As a result resentments build up over time. The partners pull farther and farther apart, and the number of topics they cannot talk about increases until they don't talk about much of anything. In the end their relationship dies.

This familiar and sad scenario will not happen to you.

Because you've done the hard work of going through this book, there isn't anything you can't talk about, and this critical skill will make all the difference in your relationship. Instead of experiencing decreasing levels of intimacy, you will experience increasing levels of closeness.

WHERE DO YOU GO FROM HERE?

The apostle Paul says in 1 Thessalonians 4:1, "We instructed you how to live in order to please God, as in fact you are living. Now we ask you and urge you in the Lord Jesus to do this more and more." Just as Paul is urging these Christians to keep growing in their relationship with Jesus, I am asking you to keep growing in your relationship with each other. You know how to do this now, so keep on doing it!

Continue to be honest about everything. If you are upset about something your partner has said or done, tell him or her. If you have a need, speak up. If you want to ask a question, ask it. If you want to offer some constructive criticism, do it lovingly. But do it. If you have a disagreement, talk it out. If your partner does or says something you appreciate and it makes you feel loved, say so. If you have the urge to kiss your partner, pucker up right then and plant a smacker.

If you can talk about any problem, you can fix it. If you can talk about any issue, you will grow closer. Every time— every time—you talk through an issue, you grow a little bit closer.

Stay honest. Stay intentional. Stay alert because a healthy relationship requires continual attention and maintenance. I promise that you will face problems and crises. We all do. I also promise that if you commit to talking through each issue, no matter how hard it is or how long it takes, your relationship with win. Together, you will grow stronger and stronger and closer and closer.

ADDITIONAL RESOURCES

*O*THER BOOKS BY David Clarke:

❧ *Married but Lonely: Seven Steps You Can Take With or Without Your Spouse's Help*, with William G. Clarke

❧ *What Happened to Happily Ever After? Fix the Top Ten Mistakes Most Couples Make*, with William G. Clarke

❧ *I Don't Want a Divorce: A 90-Day Guide to Saving Your Marriage*, with William G. Clarke

❧ *What to Do When He Says, "I Don't Love You Anymore": An Action Plan to Regain Confidence, Power, and Control*

❧ *Kiss Me Like You Mean It: Solomon's Crazy in Love How-To Manual*

❧ *A Marriage After God's Own Heart*

❧ *Men Are Clams, Women Are Crowbars: Understand Your Differences and Make Them Work*

❧ *Winning the Parenting War: A Battle Plan for Securing Victory on the Home Front*

🙖 *I'm Not OK and Neither Are You: The Six Steps to Emotional Freedom*

🙖 *The Top Ten Most Outrageous Couples of the Bible*, with William G. Clarke

To schedule a seminar, order Dr. Clarke's books, set up an in-person or telephone advice session, schedule a marriage intensive, or access his speaking schedule, please contact:

David Clarke Seminars

www.davidclarkeseminars.com

1-888-516-8844

or

Marriage & Family Enrichment Center

6505 North Himes Avenue

Tampa, Florida 33614

ABOUT THE AUTHORS

David E. Clarke, PhD, is a Christian psychologist and speaker and the author of ten books, including *Married but Lonely* and *What Happened to Happily Ever After?* A graduate of Dallas Theological Seminary and Western Conservative Baptist Seminary in Portland, Oregon, he has been in private practice for over thirty years. He and his wife, Sandy, live in Tampa, Florida, and have four children and two grandchildren.

William G. Clarke, MA, has been a marriage and family therapist for over thirty years. He is a graduate of the University of Southern California and the California Family Study Center, where he earned his master's degree. With his wife, Kathleen, he served with Campus Crusade for Christ (CRU) for nine years. He is the founder of the Marriage and Family Enrichment Center in Tampa, Florida.

CONNECT WITH US!

CHARISMA HOUSE

(Spiritual Growth)

- Facebook.com/CharismaHouse
- @CharismaHouse
- Instagram.com/CharismaHouse

SILOAM

(Health)

- Pinterest.com/CharismaHouse

MEV MODERN ENGLISH VERSION

(Bible)
www.mevbible.com